WILL THEIR EGOS DRIVE HUMANS TO EXTINCTION?

Humans Are Seemingly Unable to Control Their Selves

A reflection on the human condition and the horrendous costs of human ignorance and unbridled ego

"Only the man who can impose discipline on himself is fit to discipline others or can impose discipline on others."
William A. Feather (8/25/1889 - 1/7/1981)

"Those who cannot remember the past are condemned to repeat it."
George Santayana (12/16/1863 - 9/26/1952)

DAVID L. R. STEIN

PAGE PUBLISHING, INC.
New York, NY

First originally published by Page Publishing, Inc. 2019

ISBN 978-1-64462-241-4 (Paperback)
ISBN 978-1-64462-242-1 (Digital)

Printed in the United States of America

CONTENTS

PREFACE

What is it about humankind that prevents them from eliminating their recurrent crimes, wars, and social regressions? While the question may appear to be academic, if an answer could be found, it could herald a new era in which all the human energy, resources, and talents which are currently expended in wasteful crimes, wars, and social regressions instead could be invested in improving the human condition.

Sadly, throughout history human behavior seems to reflect an implicit assumption that no such program is possible, not to mention practical. What is the origin of such pessimism? When Shakespeare wrote "what's past is prologue[1]," was he simply reflecting conventional wisdom? And, if so, what was the source of that wisdom, and why is it still accepted by some as incontrovertible truth?

The answer appears to be that acceptance of an unknowable future is intolerable to what is known in Freudian psychoanalytic theory as the human "ego[2]" or "self[3]." Consequently, the primitive human ego conjures a future which is acceptable to itself and, for lack of an alternative, simply improvises by assuming the unknowable future can't be much different from what is knowable—i.e., the past.

While that may satisfy a primitive and uneducated human ego, it's little comfort to those with a knowledge of human history. Consequently, some of those still troubled by fears of an uncertain future find solace in world religions forecasting an "end time[4]" while promising immortality to the devout and the redeemed. That leaves agnostics and atheists in a quandary and explains their many desperate attempts to create a totalitarian Neo-Marxist utopia through social engineering—which attempts, without exception, have been unmitigated disasters to date.

It's the thesis of this book that what has prevented humankind from making uninterrupted social progress is a historically demonstrated inability of humankind to control their selves—i.e., to adequately restrain their innate animalism. Examinations of multiple sources of human political and social instability all reflect an evident inability to overcome innate human territoriality and xenophobia exacerbated by egocentricity and ignorance. Many sages have long believed, as Einstein and the ancient Greeks apparently did, that such weaknesses are humanly insurmountable as a consequence of humankind's innate animalism. Of course such a conclusion easily could become a self-fulfilling prophesy and leaves unanswered the question of why their innate animalism can't be restrained by humankind's better judgment—i.e., by their "superegos[5]."

Yet, human societal evolution, or lack of it, over the last one hundred years is a cause for grave concern. Indeed, some of today's US students—marching in the streets, attacking any who dare to disagree with them, destroying private and public property, proclaiming they are what they are not, and sowing sedition everywhere they go with seeming impunity—are reminiscent of nothing so much as the *Sturmabteilung*[6] of 1930s Germany. Moreover, the undeclared "stealth war" that has been waged by China against the US over the last sixty-nine years bears a strong resemblance to the actions of 1930s Japan. Evidently, the geopolitical forces operating in today's world are little different from those which operated one hundred years ago.

Hopefully, past is not prologue, and human societies may yet evolve to a point where all human children will receive sufficient parenting and trustworthy education in their formative years to enable their better judgment to restrain their innate animalism. It's not too much to hope for, and it would put a glorious end to recurrent debilitating and self-defeating social regressions engineered by self-appointed, self-aggrandizing, self-perpetuating, self-righteous, self-serving, and supercilious political "elites."

Praemonitus praemunitus—"forewarned is forearmed"— the motto of the US Army

INTRODUCTION

In a real sense, the human animal well may be its own worst enemy. With each successive generation seemingly unable to learn from the mistakes and successes of its predecessors, humans persist in recurrent backsliding from periods of social progress into periods of social regression. Whatever the cause of humanity's historical failure to make steady and uninterrupted social progress, it's the root cause of all human strife which does not result directly from forces beyond humanity's control. Accordingly, it behooves humankind to gain an understanding of this fateful human deficiency so it can be minimized if not completely eliminated.

"We are moving toward a dictatorship of relativism which does not recognize anything as for certain and which has as its highest goal one's own ego and one's own desires."[1]—Pope Benedict XVI[7]

Nothing illustrates the truth of Pope Benedict XVI's pessimistic assessment better than humanity's persistence in denying its animal nature as exemplified by the World Transformation Movement[8] (WTM), a cult which grew out of the musings of Australian biologist Jeremy Griffith[9].

"How do we account for humans' aggressive and competitive nature? It is a question that has tormented humanity since time immemorial...the excuse that our behavior is due to 'savage animal instincts' doesn't stack up because...we suffer from the conscious-mind-based, PSYCHOLOGICALLY [sic] troubled human condition, not the genet-

---

[1] *Benedict vs. the Dictatorship of Relativism*[10]

ic-opportunism-based, animal condition. And what's more, our instincts are to be cooperative and loving, not competitive and aggressive…Jeremy explains that this conflict between our intellect and instincts caused our species to become psychologically defensive, angry, alienated and egocentric—the aggressive and competitive state we refer to as the human condition. And with the ability now to explain this conflict, all those insecure, defensive behaviors are obsoleted, brought to an end—we are freed from the human condition!"[2]

Could life be any sweeter than that? If we accept Griffith's Pollyannaish assessment, we can all go back to our slumber like the hapless Eloi in H. G. Wells'[11] novel *THE TIME MACHINE*[12] secure in the knowledge the world will take care of itself due to the "cooperative and loving" nature of the human animal.

Or can we? Compare Griffith's assessment with that of Albert Einstein[13] in his 74th year.

"The existence and validity of human rights are not written in the stars. The ideals concerning the conduct of men toward each other and the desirable structure of the community have been conceived and taught by enlightened individuals in the course of history. Those ideals and convictions which resulted from historical experience, from the craving for beauty and harmony, have been readily accepted in theory by man—and at all times, have been trampled upon by the same people under the pressure of their animal instincts. A large part of history is therefore replete with the struggle for those human rights, an eternal struggle in which a final victory can never be won. But to tire in that struggle would mean the ruin of society."[3]

Can humans rise above their innate animalism to minimize, if not completely eliminate, recurrent crimes, wars, and social regressions? Apparently, Griffith believes they can. Or, was Einstein cor-

---

[2] *The explanation of the human condition*[14]

[3] *Human Rights*,[15] Address to the Chicago Decalogue Society, February 20, 1954

rect? Is humanity destined to suffer a perpetual series of feckless attempts to preserve its human rights as a consequence of its innate animalism? And, given humanity's penchant for self-destruction and self-indulgence, will humankind eventually be the instrument of their own extinction?

WHAT IS MEANT BY EGO AND SUPEREGO?

Merriam-Webster's Unabridged Dictionary defines ego as "*the largely conscious part of the personality* [i.e., mind] *that is derived from the id through contacts with reality and that mediates the demands of the id, of the superego, and of external everyday reality in the interest of preserving the organism.*" Note the word "organism" suggests that animals other than humans can have egos.

"*According to <u>Sigmund Freud's</u>*[16] *psychoanalytic theory, there are three parts to the personality: the ego, the id and the superego. The ego is the psychological component of the personality that is represented by our conscious decision-making process. The id is the instinctual, biological component, and the superego is the social component of our personality and conscience. Our behavior is determined by the interaction of these three components…*

The ego is the second component of personality to develop, usually around the ages of two to three years old [i.e., for humans]. *The ego is responsible for sorting out what is real. It helps us make sense of our thoughts and the world around us. It is the component of our personality we are aware of the most. This is because the ego is the part that controls our consciousness.*"[4]

Merriam-Webster's Unabridged Dictionary defines superego as "*a major sector of the psyche* [i.e., mind] *that is mostly unconscious but partly conscious, that develops out of the ego by internalization or*

---

4   <u>The Ego: Definition & Examples</u>[17]

introjection in response to advice, threats, warnings, and punishment especially by parents but also by teachers and other authority, that reflects parental conscience and the rules of society, and that serves as an aid in character formation and as a protector for the ego against overwhelming id impulses."

Accordingly, the superego is a self-control mechanism developed later in life through acquisition of real life experience—i.e., education—which enables the ego to accommodate unavoidable realities as they are encountered—which, if they were ignored, might jeopardize an individual's welfare. Those who are familiar with the taming of wild mammals—e.g., the breaking of horses—or the training of untrained mammals—e.g., dogs—will recognize the similarity with "the terrible twos" in human children and their gradual development of self-control through "advice, threats, warnings, and punishment [i.e., discipline]."

"He who gains a victory over other men is strong; but he who gains a victory over himself is all powerful."[5]—Laozi[18] (c. 600 BCE)

From their definitions, it's clear that egos are inherent sources of conflict which can inhibit socializing with others, and superegos are needed to override instinctive antisocial reactions to an individual's environment which could be, and frequently would be, counterproductive to its own welfare. Preventing such potentially dangerous and counterproductive instinctive reactions requires timely acquisition of a superego. Thus, egos are essential for survival, and superegos are essential for acceptable social behavior and greater success in life.

As both egos and superegos are self-preservation mechanisms, it's fair to conclude that all social mammals must have at least primitive egos and superegos to survive and learn from their life experiences. It's not surprising then that humans suffering from stunted superegos emulate the behaviors of other mammals by limiting their social interactions with other members of their own species through self-segregation in relatively homogeneous cliques, cults, families,

---

[5]   AZ Quotes[19]

gangs, neighborhoods, and similar self-identifying groups. In the case of sociopathic personalities suffering from extremely stunted superegos, group size can be reduced to single individuals, who then necessarily become engaged in a self-perceived <u>Hobbesian War</u>[20].

Counterintuitively, many mammals including humans are known to adopt strangers— sometimes even members of other species—into their groups. Evidently, group admissions and exclusions are not based on ethnicity or race but on acceptance of a non-threatening common culture—providing a totally satisfactory explanation of why multiculturalism inevitably leads to ostracism and <u>Balkanization</u>[21].

THE IMPORTANCE OF A HIGHLY DEVELOPED SUPEREGO

Unfortunately, highly developed superegos are not essential for survival and therein lies the source of much human tragedy. Human egos provide the driving force that animates us all. Yet, egocentricity—i.e., egos run amok in the absence of adequately developed superegos—are the wellspring of all human evil and the cause of much of human strife. What is the source of such human egocentricity? The short answer is that humans are born *tabla rasa*, and human egocentricity is the inevitable result of inadequate parenting and failure to properly educate young people to the realities of life and the world in which they live—which are a *sine qua non* for development of robust superegos.

"Childish egocentrism [i.e., egocentricity] is, in its essence, an inability to differentiate between the ego and the social environment."[6]—Jean Piaget[22]

The Freudian psychoanalytic model as first proposed was a topographical model which separated the human mind into three parts, namely: a conscious part, a preconscious part, and an unconscious part. However, Freud later abandoned the topographical model in favor of a structural model[23] which defines both the ego and superego as partly conscious and partly unconscious. The dis-

---

[6] Brainy Quote[24]

tinction between conscious and unconscious human behavior is important, and it helps to explain why people exhibit two different kinds of self-respect.

The first kind of self-respect to be developed is a primitive kind which is derived from the primitive superego, is largely unconscious, and is evident even among small children. The second kind of self-respect which is developed later in life is an educated kind of self-respect which is derived from an educated superego, is largely conscious, and is not evident until late adolescence at the earliest. As a product of an educated superego, educated self-respect continues to grow throughout the lifetimes of healthy individuals.

Interestingly, as suicide represents the ultimate failure of self-respect, educated self-respect provides a totally adequate explanation of why suicide rates are higher among the young, the ignorant, and the losers in life's game than they are among better educated and more successful adults. Thus, suicide rates can be viewed as direct measures of the relative failure or success of the parenting and education needed for development of robust superegos.

One does not need to be religious to recognize the profound truth in the biblical proverb[25] "*He that spareth his rod hateth his son: but he that loveth him chasteneth him betimes.*" Frequently, misquoted as "spare the rod and spoil the child[26]," the metaphor is the same. Nor does one need to be a moralist or a psychologist to recognize that egocentricity and psychological hedonism are inherently self-destructive, as that reality is constantly on display among human criminal populations and other losers in life's game. However, to fully comprehend why egocentricity and psychological hedonism are inherently self-destructive, one needs to understand the links between parental discipline, childhood maturation, educational achievement, and self-respect.

What is not found in ancient religious proverbs is that inadequate childhood discipline ineluctably results in less self-discipline—i.e., less developed superegos; less self-discipline ineluctably results in less self-respect; and less self-respect ineluctably results in more self-destructive behaviors. Accordingly, childhood discipline is not only a *sine qua non* for development of a healthy superego, and hence acceptable social behavior and greater success in life, but it's also a *sine qua non* for development of sufficient self-respect to restrain self-destructive behaviors.

It's hardly surprising then that the combination of a decline in childhood discipline and adult moral values, increased affluence and self-indulgence, and the retrograde political corruption of educational institutions over the last one hundred years have led to generations of egocentric and hedonistic adolescents intent on self-indulgence and little else.

The Importance of Parenting

Due to their greater intelligence, human animals have a greater capacity for mischief—as reflected in the aphorism "idle hands are the devil's workshop"—and consequently a greater need to acquire extensive knowledge of socially acceptable and socially unacceptable human behaviors, or "historical experience" in Einstein's parlance.

Rudimentary superegos are sufficient for survival of less-intelligent mammals, but greater human intelligence brings with it a greater capacity for deception and a resultant requirement for more robust superegos. More specifically, human guile and ingenuity permit evil to be camouflaged as good and good to be camouflaged as evil, the important to be camouflaged as unimportant and the unimportant to be camouflaged as important, the moral to be camouflaged as immoral and the immoral to be camouflaged as moral, right to be camouflaged as wrong and wrong to be camouflaged as right, what is true to be camouflaged as false and what is false to be camouflaged as true, etc. Consequently, to survive and prosper in the real world, humans require timely acquisition of knowledge which will assist them in discriminating between what is evil and what is good, what is important and what is unimportant, what is moral and what is immoral, what is right and what is wrong, what is true and what is false, etc.

Moral strictures as well as civil and criminal laws designed to control the excesses of egocentric human behaviors which could offend or harm one's fellow humans—such as assault and battery, compulsive gambling, drug addiction, fraud, murder, promiscuous sexual behavior, theft, etc.—are essential to public welfare. Of course, none of these laws or strictures are effective unless human children are disciplined in them in a timely manner so they can be fully absorbed and incorporated into children's developing superegos. Sadly, human affluence and technology confer an increased ability to shield children from the harsh realities which are essential to development of healthy superegos.

The coddling of children which shields them from harsh realities and its resultant diminution of parental discipline, guidance, and training inevitably results in extended adolescence and retarded superego development. In this regard, the lack of parental discipline engendered by the misguided teachings of Benjamin Spock[27]—i.e., insistence on enabling immediate self-gratification and facilitation of a complete unwillingness to exercise self-control and self-restraint—are perhaps the greatest impediments to the healthy development, education, and maturation of children yet conceived. Based as they are on denial of humankind's innate animalism, the teachings of Benjamin Spock are as counterproductive, ignorant, and naive as those of Jeremy Griffith.

Other factors contributing to the stunted superegos of many of today's adolescents include extreme poverty and extreme affluence. Extreme poverty frequently results in a breakdown of the nuclear family in which children are typically raised in the absence of one or both of their biological parents. In such cases, the nominal parent is frequently unable to provide the discipline needed for healthy development of children's superegos—with the result that their wards often exhibit feral behaviors. Additionally, the divorce of affluent parents can result in a breakdown of the nuclear family via creation of single-parent households in which the resident parent is frequently unable to provide the discipline needed for healthy development of children's superegos—with the result that children raised in affluent single-parent households often exhibit feral behaviors similar to those who grow up in extreme poverty[28].

On the other hand, extreme affluence affords parents the opportunity to "spoil" their children by showering them with lavish gifts, toys, and luxuries while shielding them from the harsh realities of the world in which they live. While frequently motivated by their parents' sense of guilt for their not being able to spend more time with their children, this unfortunate practice engenders a sense of entitlement in their children which builds on intrinsic egocentricity and narcissism unrestrained by primitive superegos.

Historically, religion played a significant role in the moral disciplining of children. However, the decline of religion[29] in the Western world has dramatically reduced the moral disciplining of children, and the void has not been filled by either parents or secular educational institutions. Consequently, each successive generation in the Western world has grown up with less moral discipline, less self-discipline, and less self-respect than prior generations. The result has been that a larger share of each succeeding generation has grown up without the moral discipline, self-discipline, and self-respect needed to restrain egocentric, psychologically hedonistic, and self-destructive behaviors.

Inevitably, an increasing percentage of children in the Western world have grown up somewhat wild with stunted superegos and little understanding of their own flawed—albeit human—nature. To turn such animals loose on society is to invite the kinds of social tragedies now unfolding in our schools and on our streets—where children are not only exposed to the worst examples of juvenile behavior, but all-too-frequently acquire the unrestrained behavior patterns of the dregs of society allowed to run amok in their midst—and learn little or nothing constructive to a healthy superego in the process.

Adolescent humans with mature bodies and immature minds afflicted with stunted superegos present real dangers to human society. Anyone who has worked with mammals large enough to be a threat to humans well knows that, without adequately developed superegos to restrain their innate animalism, humans are vastly more dangerous—both to themselves and to others—than are most wild mammals. Unsurprisingly, the coddling of children which shields them from harsh realities inevitably results in increased crime and juvenile delinquency.

The Importance of Education

While proper parenting provides a necessary foundation for the acquisition of real-world knowledge, parenting by itself is insufficient preparation for adult success in technologically-advanced societies. Due to the fact that technologies change rapidly, those encountered by the next generation are frequently unknown to prior generations. Hence, in today's world, continuing life-long learning is increasingly important to the acquisition of real-world knowledge.

Sadly, some observers who have noted the smug conceit of self-proclaimed "elites" in the US today might get the mistaken impression that those with a higher education naturally exhibit exaggerated egocentricity and over-confidence, if not outright contempt for the less-educated. In reality, nothing could be further from the truth. All who have pursued their educations far enough to qualify as having acquired a bona fide higher education will agree with Henning W. Prentis, Jr.[30] who summed it up as follows.

"If I were asked to pick out the one paramount blessing of a college education, I think I should place mental humility above all others. Hence it has always seemed to me that every student should pursue at least one subject far enough to realize how little he can ever hope to know about it when he compared his own proficiency with that of the real master minds in that particular field."[7]

Those who claim an elite status simply because they have college degrees are demonstrating a serious want of higher education. The difference is not between those who have college degrees and those who don't. The difference is between those who recognize the limitations of their own knowledge and those who don't. The former

---

[7]   The Cult of Competency,[31] by Henning W. Prentis, Jr., Mid-Year Convocation of the General Alumni Society of the University of Pennsylvania, 1943

have acquired wisdom and with wisdom comes humility; the latter have acquired only knowledge. Just as wisdom is the wellspring of humility and understanding, ignorance is the wellspring of arrogance and conceit. Thus, it's not surprising that the most arrogant and conceited among us are also the most ignorant of the limitations of their own knowledge. This obvious truth has been known for enough generations to be immortalized in the appellation "learned fool" and the aphorism "a little knowledge is a dangerous thing."

Conceived as they were by Marxists [i.e., devotees of <u>Karl Marx</u>[32]] in the 1920s and 1930s, US teachers' unions were deliberately designed to undermine parental control and supervision of children for the express purpose of making students more receptive to Neo-Marxist cultural brainwashing—as well as to deprive them of knowledge of their US cultural heritage, the US constitution, and free-market capitalism. That their goal has been largely achieved is evidenced by the fact that, while <u>nearly two-thirds of the US population has at least some college education</u>[33], most have little or no understanding of US exceptionalism.

*"At vast expense, the universities channel students into echoing corridors of an increasingly reactionary educational establishment that imagines that socialist [i.e., Neo-Marxist] nostrums, identity politics, chemophobia, sterile hedonism, druidical sun-henges, totemic windmills, and great walls of batteries are **progressive**."*[8]

A similar result is sought through the so-called "politically correct," or PC, movement—which substitutes Neo-Marxist censorship and cultural brainwashing for logical argument and rational discourse. An outgrowth of the Neo-Marxist take-over of US educational institutions effected in the last one hundred years, the PC movement has become increasingly pernicious through dissemination of its lies and seditious agitprop via mass media. Consequently,

---

[8]   *LIFE AFTER GOOGLE*[34]/ *The Fall of Big Data and the Rise of the Blockchain Economy,* by George Gilder, Gateway Editions, Kindle Edition, 2018

PC falsehoods now permeate academic textbooks, Internet postings, magazines, movies, newspapers, radio, television, and theatre.

Comparing the sale of indulgences by the Holy Roman Catholic Church in the sixteenth century to the current US practice of inducing everyone to acquire a college education, irrespective of the cost, the 1517 Fund[35]—a Peter Thiel[36] spinoff—thoroughly condemns the practice as deceitful institutionalized extortion. George Gilder[37] summarizes the indictment as follows.

"The fund's name alludes to another historic decentralization, launched on October 31, 1517. That was the day that Martin Luther posted his Ninety-five Theses on the church door at Wittenberg. Among the abuses Luther was protesting was the selling of indulgences. The remission of the temporal penalty due to sins, an indulgence, like other spiritual goods, must not be sold. The pardoners who perpetrated this abuse would issue a document memorializing the transaction. The 1517 Fund explains the parallel: 'Likewise, universities today are selling a piece of paper at great cost and telling people that buying it is the only way they can save their souls. Universities call it a diploma, and they're making a fortune doing it. Call us heretical if you like, but the 1517 Fund is dedicated to dispelling that paper illusion.'

The Thiel Fellowships and the 1517 Fund are protesting the layers on layers of government grants that impose a stifling conformity on our universities through the indoctrination there of a single [i.e., Neo-Marxist] system of the world. Above all, they denounce the horrendous debt load of more than $1.5 trillion—roughly 7 percent of the US gross domestic product—heaped on the hapless American [i.e., US] student to pay for a bloated academic establishment, debt that has driven whole generations out of the entrepreneurial economy that enriched their forebears and endowed the universities themselves...

The academy, already a wealthy pillar of the American establishment, receives with its ideology a sense of entitlement to government support. While tuition and other educational costs soared for decades at multiples faster than inflation and most graduates' incomes languished, the universities blithely funded their enrichment on the backs of ever more indebted students. Loaded down with debt, young people eschew entrepreneurial activities and even marriage. As business starts stagnate in America, they drift toward socialist dependency."[9]

Unfortunately, incompetent and misguided parenting together with politically-corrupted educational and governmental institutions have combined to produce extended adolescence and retarded superego development of US children. These unfortunate results of a failing social order create or exacerbate a host of other social problems—such as growing drug cultures, juvenile delinquency, religious cults, street gangs, and political and social extremism—which well may require corresponding adjustments to social restraints.

The 1980s increase in the US legal drinking age is an example of the kind of adjustment to social restraints now needed to accommodate the later maturation of US children, which well may portend the need for other adjustments as well. For example, the extended adolescence of US children and their consequent unwillingness to accept adult responsibilities has resulted in a prolonged economic dependence on their parents as well as postponement of marriage and family responsibilities.

"The most striking feature of American [i.e., US] family formation today is how late marriage takes place. The median age of first marriage of American men in 1991 was 26.3, up almost four years from the historic low of 22.5 recorded in the mid-1950s... For women, the figures today are even more striking: The 1993 median was 24.1 years, the highest average age of marriage ever recorded for American women. Although well over 90 percent of American men and women eventually do marry, postponed matrimony has become the norm...

Delayed marriage is by no means unique to America, and similar patterns can be found throughout advanced industrial nations."[10]

---

[9] Gilder, op cit

[10] *CHANGING SOCIETIES*[38]*/ Essential Sociology for Our Times*, by Anthony M. Orum, John W. C. Johnstone, and Stephanie Riger, Rowman & Littlefield Publishers, 1999

These well may be healthy changes as the human brain is not fully developed until age twenty-five[39] in any case. However, they do raise the question of whether or not corresponding adjustments should be made to social restraints. For example, a corresponding increase in the legal voting age—say from 21 to 25—may be merited to prevent a growing share of the electorate from being largely ignorant of the harsh realities of the world in which they live and, consequently, woefully unprepared to participate in the management of world affairs.

Sadly, many humans never achieve full adult maturity. While the self-control and self-respect of healthy individuals continue to grow throughout their lifetimes, many decades can be required for humans to acquire extensive knowledge of socially acceptable and socially unacceptable human behaviors, or "historical experience."

"A study conducted by Hopwood et al[11] presented that trait stability increases with age… It is agreed though that personality stability peaks quite late into adulthood, even later than would be expected. A recent meta-analysis found that it is not until after the age of 50 that there are significant levels of personality trait stability."[12]

One does not need a familiarity with fictional stories like _LORD OF THE FLIES_[40] or the Star Trek episode _And the Children Shall Lead_[41] to appreciate the inherent dangers in a world ruled by humans with mature bodies and immature minds afflicted with stunted superegos. Failure to restore competent parenting, to reform failing educational and governmental institutions, and to make corresponding adjustments to social restraints is to invite social disasters—including, but not limited to, social regressions.

---

[11] Hopwood, C. J., Donnellan, M. B., Blonigen, D. M., Krueger, R. F., McGue, M., Iacono, W. G., & Burt, S. A. (2011). _Genetic and environmental influences on personality trait stability and growth during the transition to adulthood:_[42] A three-wave longitudinal study. Journal of Personality and Social Psychology, 100(3), 545-556

[12] _Models of Maturity: The effect of maturity on personality trait stability_[43]

SIGNIFICANT SOURCES OF POLITICAL AND SOCIAL INSTABILITY

Ecocide and Genocide

Humans have been thoughtlessly changing, destroying, and polluting their own habitats from time immemorial. Examples include: heavy metals pollution resulting from the cupellation smelting process[44], creation of an arid "dust bowl[45]" in central North America resulting from over-cultivation of huge tracts of semiarid prairie, destruction of the Aral Sea[46] from over-diversion of source water for irrigation, the Chernobyl Exclusion Zone[47] resulting from human managerial incompetence, and many others[48].

In the process, humans have been changing, destroying, and polluting the habitats of many other species in addition to their own. Insolent and wanton habitat destruction in combination with the over-harvesting of animal and plant species needed by humans to sustain themselves has ravaged other species for thousands of years. Examples of animal species driven to extinction include: megafauna[49] around the world, the Dodo bird[50], Passenger pigeon[51], bison[52], and hundreds of other species. Examples of decimated animal species on the verge of extinction include: Beluga sturgeon[53], elephants, Huchen[54] (Danube salmon), and many others[55].

While the history of Easter Island[56] is somewhat controversial, there is general agreement that its habitat was virtually destroyed by its human inhabitants. Prevailing opinion is that an otherwise heavily forested tropical paradise was systematically devastated in as little as a few hundred years[57] through a combination of human overpopulation, over-use of otherwise perpetually renewable resources, and pollution—all of which produced a hellish environment that inevitably led to tribal warfare, starvation, and human cannibalism[58].

All who are familiar with the history of Easter Island likely will agree that it represents an object lesson for humanity in what not to do. Yet, there is scant evidence, if any, that humanity has learned the lesson of Easter Island. All around the world humankind continue to demonstrate colossal ecological ignorance and an insolent and wanton disregard for judicious long-term management of natural resources—as demonstrated by the continuing destruction, exhaustion, and pollution of otherwise perpetually renewable resources, as well as a continuing lack of recycling and an attendant exhaustion of finite natural resources.

Such unfettered resource exhaustion would be bad enough, but humankind also continue to demonstrate an insolent and wanton disregard of the need to maintain a healthy human habitat as well. For example, humans continue to pollute air, earth, and water[59] with agricultural and industrial chemicals, human garbage, trash, and waste. Moreover, humans continue to adulterate their own foodstuffs with unnecessary additives, such as colorings, drugs, flavorings, and preservatives; and we even continue to pollute earth's spatial environment with abandoned exploratory space vehicles, satellites, and other space debris[60].

What other than egocentricity and ignorance—i.e., hubris and stupidity—can explain humanity's pollution of its own habitat to such an extent that it becomes unsafe for animal and plant life, thereby transforming what could be, and should be, perpetual sources of renewable life-sustaining resources into dangerous hazards to life. Clearly, some human behaviors must change if humanity is to halt its historical insolent and wanton destruction of its natural habitat—of the kind which led to ecocide, genocide, and the near extinction of the inhabitants of Easter Island.

Religion and Genocide

Those who are devoutly religious believe their destinies are controlled by supernatural forces beyond human comprehension and put their faith in deities who promise them immortality if only they abide by their religious teachings. But is that an intellectually respectable thing to do? How convenient it is to believe we humans are impotent to affect our own destinies—as it excuses us from making any serious and sustained effort to stop actions, habits, and practices which could be counterproductive to our well-being and could even threaten extinction of the human species.

"Neither can I nor would I want to conceive of an individual that survives his physical death; let feeble souls, from fear or absurd egoism, cherish such thoughts."[13]

And, while avoiding responsibility for their own actions well may be a great source of comfort for many, it has the unfortunate consequence of promising immortality to humans independently of their actions while living on this earth. Why then worry about human corruption, crime, decadence, depravity, evil, and licentiousness at all? Is not the same eternal after-life promised to every devoutly religious person? Could life be any more wonderful than that?

To be sure, in addition to promising immortality or "heaven" to those who abide by their religious teachings, some religions promise eternal suffering or "hell" to those who fail to live up to them. But all religions are not so demanding, and even those promising both heaven and hell provide means for redemption and even death-bed absolution. Consequently, the positive rewards of living a devout life always outrank the punishments for not doing so.

Moreover, it's difficult to overlook the fact that religions in and of themselves can be sources of human conflicts and devastation[61]. Nor is it possible to overlook the disastrous retrograde consequences which some religious cults and sects have had throughout human

---

[13] Albert Einstein Quotes on Life After Death[62]

history. Furthermore, when religion competes for political power as it's want to do, it fails to be a source of enlightenment and instead becomes a source of social discord, dysfunction, and instability. Perhaps the most egregious example is Islamist[63] extremism which actively promotes genocide and subordinates both civil and criminal laws to religious doctrine.

Sadly, religious faith in a promised immortality well could be simply another example of the human ego run amok in the absence of an adequately developed superego—i.e., a kind of willful blindness—which suppresses the harsh reality of human mortality to achieve a more self-pleasing result. In other words, it could be nothing more than a convenient cop-out to avoid having to come to grips with harsh reality. Are we humans guilty of such irrational behavior? Unfortunately, we are, as demonstrated by the fact that much of humanity's woeful naiveté can be explained only as demonstrations of an inability to learn based on a deliberate childlike refusal to acknowledge what is obvious to any who are unencumbered by willful blindness.

Tragically, this kind of mind-numbing blind religious faith has the power to reduce human behavior to the level of unconscious farm animals being led to their slaughter. It did not well serve the victims of five centuries of European witch trials[64], nor did it well serve the Jews during the holocaust[65] engineered by the Third Reich[66], and there is no evidence that it has ever served others any better.

Accordingly, using religion to rationalize a lack of human responsibility for human actions—especially those which could threaten extinction of the human species—is, in reality, an act of cowardice resulting from human egocentricity and ignorance. If human history to date is any indication, humankind would do well to look to themselves and not to Divine Providence[67] for salvation.

Failing Educational and Governmental Institutions

Sadly, despite the fact that the US is the greatest force for human liberty the world has yet conceived, and despite the equally compelling fact that competing Neo-Marxism—i.e., an amalgamation of all variations of Marxist-inspired totalitarian political ideologies, including socialism, communism, fascism (né national socialism), and progressivism, which is now evolving into something euphemistically termed postmodernism[68]—has achieved nothing but a consistent record of disastrous, if not monstrous, failures—including responsibility for the unnatural deaths of an estimated one hundred million people[69] in the last century alone, the US continues to be plagued by utopian Neo-Marxist pipedreams which, if pursued, would inevitably lead to surrender of the liberties for which a dozen generations of US citizens already have fought and died.

"America [i.e., the US] is the only country ever founded on an idea. The only country that is not founded on race or even common history. It's founded on an idea and the idea is liberty. That is probably the rarest phenomena in the political history of the world; this has never happened before. And not only has it happened, but it's worked. We are the most flourishing, the most powerful, most influential country on Earth with this system, invented by the greatest political geniuses probably in human history. "14—Charles Krauthammer[70]

Recognizing the novelty of their innovation, the founders of the US embarked on a deliberate high-priority campaign to educate the US electorate to the uniqueness of the US Constitution and its founding principles and values. Tragically, massive twentieth and twenty-first century immigration of illiterate and unskilled peoples from around the world possessing little or no knowledge of US founding principles and values, and the insidious and seditious promotion of Neo-Marxist indoctrination and multiculturalism by Neo-Marxist revolutionaries now dominating US educational institutions, have given rise to a US population which is increasingly ignorant of everything that has made the US "the most flourishing, the most powerful, most influential country on Earth."

By no coincidence, US educational institutions have gone from deliberately emphasizing civics and US founding principles and values

---

14 Quotation of the day on American exceptionalism...[71]

in the eighteenth and nineteenth centuries to deliberately deemphasizing them in the twentieth and twenty-first centuries. The predictable result is that US citizens and recent immigrants have never before been so ignorant of US exceptionalism and what is required to preserve it. But it wasn't always so, as evidenced by the following eloquent account excerpted from a 1943 address by Henning W. Prentis, Jr.

"I hold here a facsimile of the handbill—printed in Latin at the expense of the students—which, in accordance with long-established custom, was distributed to the audience that attended the graduating exercises of the Class of 1763. It sets forth ninety theses in grammar, rhetoric, logic, physics, metaphysics, ethics and politics which the candidates for degrees stood ready to defend in syllogistic argument against anyone who cared to challenge them. The graduating class had been prepared for this 'public disputation,' as it was called, by long and continued practice. The Provost himself usually presided over these formal arguments which were held regularly once a week during the junior and senior years... This type of training in political, philosophic and religious principles was followed by all of our colleges and universities in Colonial days. In fact, the holding of public disputations at commencement exercises continued well into the early years of the 19th Century...the men who established the American Revolution drilled themselves in the history of humanity's previous attempts at self-government; analyzed the record of successes and failures; deduced therefrom the immutable principles essential for the permanent enjoyment of freedom; built on those foundations a new nation conceived in liberty; and continued throughout their lives as articulate in its support in time of peace, as they had been its dauntless defenders in time of war. Thus the freedom we have enjoyed in America [i.e., the US] is not the fruit of fortuitous accident, of great natural resources, or of mere isolation from the tangled skein of European politics. It is the direct result of purposeful thinking and hard work. It is the child of the cult of competency—intellectual competency, physical competency, moral competency...

To remain free, we their descendants must pay the same price they paid. For freedom, as many wise men have pointed out, is not a gift from heaven. It must be won and rewon by every generation for itself.

It is not ours for the asking, as so many complacent Americans seem to think. It is ours only for the taking—through competent personal effort in support of the eternal principles on which it rests. The way to freedom has always been a rough and arduous road. It is not for weaklings. It has never remained long under the feet of those who seek first, last and always a full stomach—at the price of a questing mind and an unfettered soul! Only a competent people can build the temple of self-government. And only a competent people can keep it standing. The floods of economic depression, the frosts of class cleavage, the ice of apathy and the winds of demagoguery, are potent forces of social erosion which are never at rest. Only through constant renewal of knowledge, faith and practice of the principles of republican self-government by a competent citizenry, can the edifice of liberty be kept intact…

To preserve itself, a representative democracy [i.e., a democratic republic] *should, therefore, guard and encourage individual competency with every means at its command. For only intellectually competent men can fully discharge the responsibilities of citizenship, weigh new proposals of government against the lessons of history, and vote intelligently… Our fathers had none of the current mystical faith in the power of government—composed of men no better, no worse on the average than the rest of us—to solve all their problems…*

The right of the people to choose their own rulers; the right of all men to free speech, free assemblage and free conscience; the right of all men to work freely at lawful vocations of their own choosing. If, through intellectual, physical or moral incompetency, we permit any one of these three fundamental rights to be undermined, the ultimate fall of the American Republic [i.e., the US] *is as inevitable as the failure of the many other attempts at popular self-government which have had their little day and gone down into the night of history. To be intellectually competent, a man* [or woman] *obviously must have a storehouse of facts, the ability to think straight, mental humility, and a certain sense of the fitness of things that we in business call good judgment… The men who set up this nation were intellectually competent to defend the principles on which it was founded. If we are to preserve it, we must prove worthy of our heritage by emulating their example. The collectivists among us are never idle. They constantly chip away at the foundations of our free institutions. So every intellectually competent citizen should be equally alert; analyze every new governmental proposal in the light of history; and decide for himself whether or not it fits into the fabric of our system…*

Yet I venture to predict that if we ever do lose our freedom in America [i.e., the US], *it will be due to public ignorance of the perils involved in outright government planning and control of our economic life. All of which again demonstrates that freedom can only be had by competent men who understand the basic principles of self-government and who recognize that 'eternal vigilance **is** the price of liberty.'"* [15]

"The tree of liberty must be refreshed from time to time with the blood of patriots and tyrants." [16]—Thomas Jefferson[72]

Unsurprisingly, some immigrants do a superior job of parenting and educating their children. Notable examples include the Chinese and Israeli diasporas. One wonders whether they draw their evident drive, inspiration, and stamina from a perceived need to take responsibility for their own welfare. Ironically, if that is the case, then the ethnic oppression and ostracism they receive in their adopted homelands have the opposite effect intended by making them more resilient and stronger. As evidenced by the economic successes of such ethnic minorities and others such as World War II veterans, those who have experienced real hardships frequently take responsibility for their own welfare and strive to educate their children in a quest to free them from dependence on others. These phenomena together with insistence on acceptance of English as the single official US language and sworn allegiance to the US Constitution as requirements for US citizenship well could explain the successful assimilation of nineteenth and early twentieth-century US immigrants—which has recently been brought to a near halt by demagogues, seditionaries, and revolutionaries extolling the virtues of multiculturalism.

Evidently, those who've not been given a free ride by society frequently exhibit superior drive, inspiration, and stamina in a quest

---

[15] Prentis, op cit

[16] Extract from Thomas Jefferson to William Stephens Smith[73]

to better themselves and their descendants. Sadly, by providing sub-sistence level life styles to many at no cost to themselves, the rise of the welfare state in the twentieth century has engendered a culture of dependence which encourages ignorance and sloth. As the recipients of this well-intentioned but woefully misguided largesse assume no responsibility for their own welfare, they cultivate a sloth-like exis-tence in which there is no perceived need for parenting, education, or personal achievement. Consequently, as wards of the state, these dregs of humanity form a cesspool of human idleness and mischief which inevitably leads to rampant human corruption, crime, deca-dence, depravity, evil, and licentiousness.

New Tools for Fomenting Social Discord, Dysfunction, and Instability

In addition to a greater capacity for mischief, the greater intel-ligence of the human animal brings with it an insatiable appetite for constant mental stimulation and titillation, and consequently, a near-universal addiction to anything which will provide amusement. When coupled with the richness of modern multimedia presenta-tions, this natural appetite of the human brain causes it to absorb enormous amounts of information streaming through modern mass media. However, given the capacity for deception, guile, and ingenu-ity of its human authors, the information so acquired frequently can't be trusted to be factual or true.

Thus, to survive and prosper in the real world, humans need to constantly discriminate for themselves what part of this con-stant stream of information is to be believed and what part is not to be believed. As such discrimination is a challenging task even for well-educated adults preoccupied with mundane activities, it becomes a potent source of political and social instability when the information is disseminated by sources which can't be trusted. Sadly, this fact has been long recognized by demagogues, seditionaries, and revolutionaries—with the inevitable result that much of what is broadcast via modern mass media is what commissars of the former Soviet Union accurately termed agitprop[74] (a portmanteau for agitation and propaganda) designed to foment social discord, dysfunction, and instability.

The challenge of shielding children from demagogic, seditious, and revolutionary agitprop and providing them with an enlightened education was difficult enough when mass media were limited to motion pictures, radio broadcasts, and the printed word but, with the advent of television, the challenge became vastly greater. That reality was recognized more than fifty years ago, as demonstrated by the following excerpt from a speech given by the then chairman of the US Federal Communications Commission.

"Your industry [i.e., the TV industry] *possesses the most powerful voice in America. It has an inescapable duty to make that voice ring with intelligence and with leadership… Why is so much of television so bad?… I do not accept the idea that the present over-all programming is aimed accurately at the public taste… A rating, at best, is an indication of how many people saw what you gave them… I believe in the people's good sense and good taste, and I am not convinced that the people's taste is as low as some of you assume… Certainly, I hope you will agree that ratings should have little influence where children are concerned… If parents, teachers, and ministers conducted their responsibilities by fol-lowing the ratings* [i.e., by working to maximize their popularity], *children would have a steady diet of ice cream, school holidays, and no Sunday school."*[17]

In the twenty-first century, the combination of the Internet, digital media, and smartphones provide nonstop around-the-clock and around-the-world access to potentially mesmerizing full-motion, high-fidelity, high-resolution, color-video presentations. People, and especially children, are immersed in these new digital media to an extent which was inconceivable only twenty-five years ago. Unfortunately, responsible regulation of mass media has thus far been virtually nonexistent. The result has been that avaricious,

---

[17] Newton N. Minow,[75] *Television and the Public Interest*, speech delivered 9 May 1961 to the National Association of Broadcasters, Washington, DC

mendacious, and politically corrupt mass media have unleashed a steady stream of almost completely uncensored agitprop on their unsuspecting clients—vastly exacerbating the challenge of shielding children from demagogic, seditious, and revolutionary agitprop and providing them with an enlightened education. Given adequate parenting and trustworthy education of children in their formative years—i.e., from birth through age 25 when the human brain is fully developed, the steady stream of agitprop impinging on the human brain from mass media is not a problem. Indeed, it's a necessary prerequisite to development of a mature superego in the same manner as exposure to human pathogens is a prerequisite to development of a mature immune system.

Contrariwise, in the absence of adequate parenting and trustworthy education of children, the constant bombardment of the human brain by demagogic, seditious, and revolutionary agitprop is, without doubt, the most effective and efficient means of cultural brainwashing the masses and fomenting the kinds of social discord, dysfunction, and instability which are essential prerequisites for sedition and social revolution. That this fact was known to revolutionaries more than one hundred years ago is illustrated by the following declaration by Lenin[76].

"The communists must be prepared to make every sacrifice and, if necessary, even resort to all sorts of cunning schemes and stratagems, to employ illegal methods, to evade and conceal the truth… The practical part of communist policy is to incite one against another… My words were calculated to evoke hatred, aversion, and contempt…not to convince but to break up the ranks of the opponent, not to correct an opponent's mistake but to destroy him, to wipe his organization off the face of the earth. This formulation is indeed of such a nature as to evoke the worst thoughts, the worst suspicions about the opponent."[18]

As evidenced by the absurdities now unfolding daily in US grammar schools, high schools, colleges, and universities, Neo-Marxists—

---

[18] Dezinformatsiya[77]

following the playbook developed by Marx, Lenin, Hitler[78], and Alinsky[79]—have largely succeeded in a complete take-over of US educational institutions[80] and mass media. Tragically, this subversive campaign has been building for more than one hundred years[81], yet it goes unrecognized by the vast majority of US citizens. Moreover, its evil and pernicious purpose is now actively aided and abetted by a majority of US mass media, which reflect generations of Neo-Marxist cultural brainwashing by failing US parental, educational, and governmental institutions—making an absurd mockery of Thomas Carlyle's[82] naive and overly optimistic view of a press corps as a kind of Fourth Estate[83].

Ever since creation of the Comintern[84] in March 1919, foreign enemies of the US have been propagandizing and proselytizing US citizens in attempts to interfere in US internal affairs. That is not new. What is new is that digital media networks are not limited by geography—thereby providing foreign enemies with an entirely new low-cost capability to subject innocent and unsuspecting US citizens of all ages to steady streams of disinformation[85].

Those old enough to recall World War II will recall the radio broadcasts by "Axis Sally" and "Tokyo Rose" designed to demoralize US troops. Sadly, in today's world, the new digital media networks ensure the same kind of disinformation is wittingly and unwittingly broadcast around the world on a daily basis. Thus, the new digital media networks have birthed an entirely new type of cybernetic warfare which poses a powerful and unprecedented threat to the political and social stability of the US—as well as any country in which a high percentage of its citizens has Internet access. That unfortunate reality was convincingly demonstrated during the 2016 US Presidential election when foreign disinformation campaigns were ramped up in the US. Tragically, the US government agencies charged with combatting cybernetic attacks and alerting US citizens to any such disinformation campaigns by foreign powers—not to mention the technocratic "elites" who own the privately held "self-regulated" US mass media networks involved—failed to perceive what was happening, and the cybernetic attacks went largely undetected, unchallenged, and unreported at the time.

Technocratic "Elites"—Social Benefactors or Egocentric Revolutionaries?

Nothing illustrates the monumental conceit of today's self-appointed technocratic "elites" better than the unbounded arrogance and hubris on display at the <u>Beneficial AI 2017</u>[86] conference sponsored by the <u>Future of Life Institute</u>[87] and held at the <u>Asilomar Conference Grounds</u>[88] in Pacific Grove, California. As related by George Gilder in *LIFE AFTER GOOGLE*, the assembled worthies had the supercilious conceit to proclaim that machines driven by their brilliantly engineered artificial intelligence, or AI, not only could, but likely would, evolve to a place of supremacy over humankind. With acid sarcasm, Gilder sums up their elitist views as follows.

"According to many prestigious voices, the industry is rapidly approaching a moment of 'singularity.' Its supercomputers in the 'Cloud' are becoming so much more intelligent than you and command such a complete sensorium of multidimensional data streams from your brain and body that you will want these machines to take over most of the decisions in your life. Advanced artificial intelligence and breakthroughs in biological codes are persuading many researchers that organisms such as human beings are simply the product of an algorithm. Inscribed in DNA and neural network logic, this algorithm can be interpreted and controlled through machine learning…

The Cloud computing and big data of companies such as Google, with its 'Deep Mind' AI, can excel individual human brains in making key life decisions… This self-learning software will also be capable of performing most of your jobs. The new digital world may not need you anymore… Don't take offense. In all likelihood, you can retire on an income which we regard as satisfactory for you. Leading Silicon Valley employers…deem most human beings unemployable because they are intellectually inferior to AI algorithms… In the past, this kind of talk of human gods, omniscience, and elite supremacy over hoi polloi may have been mostly confined to late-night bibulous blather or to mental institutions. As Silicon Valley passed through the late years of the 2010s with most of its profits devolving to Google, Apple, and Facebook, however, it appeared to be undergoing a nervous breakdown, manifested on one level by delusions of omnipotence and transcendence and on another by twitchy sieges of 'security' instructions on consumers' devices."[19]

For those who have not lived among the self-exalting "elites" of Silicon Valley, Gilder goes on to explain the origin of their fantasies and pipedreams. Indoctrinated in Neo-Marxism as they have been through their attendance at today's "finest" academies and universities, his assessment of these egocentric "elites"—as summarized here—should surprise no one.

"… Silicon Valley seems to have adopted what can best be described as a Neo-Marxist political ideology and technological vision. You may wonder how I can depict as 'Neo-Marxists' those who on the surface seem to be the most avid and successful capitalists on the planet. Marxism is much discussed as a vessel of revolutionary grievances, workers' uprisings, divestiture of chains, critiques of capital, catalogs of classes, and usurpation of the means of production. At its heart, however, the first Marxism espoused a belief that the industrial revolution of the nineteenth century solved for all time the fundamental problem of production… Marx was typical of intellectuals in imagining that his own epoch was the final stage of human history. <u>William F. Buckley</u>[89] used to call it an immanentized eschaton, a belief the 'last things' were taking place in one's own time. The Neo-Marxism of today's Silicon Valley titans repeats the error of the old Marxists in its belief that today's technology…is the definitive human achievement. The algorithmic eschaton renders obsolete not only human labor but the human mind as well…

All this is temporal provincialism and myopia, exaggerating the significance of the attainments of their own era, of their own companies, of their own special philosophies and chimeras—of themselves, really… AI is believed to be redefining what it means to be human, much as Darwin's On the Origin of Species did in its time. While Darwin [i.e., <u>Charles Darwin</u>[90]] made man just another animal, a precariously risen ape, Google-Marxism sees men as inferior intellectually to the company's

---

own algorithmic machines… What tribute to one's transformative brilliance could be more thrilling than the warning that your inventions threaten to attain consciousness and reduce human beings to patronized pets? The Asilomar Statement of AI Principles, signed by eight thousand scientists, representing a 97 percent consensus—including a passel of Nobel laureates and Hawking [i.e., <u>Stephen Hawking</u>[91]]*—echoed the billowy affirmations of Google's own 'Do No Evil'* [i.e., <u>Don't Be Evil</u>[92]] *precepts and the statement of principles of <u>Burning Man</u>*[93]… *All these pursuits reflect a breakdown of terrestrial intelligence. The intellectuals of this era are simply blind to the reality of consciousness. Consciousness is who we are, how we think, and how we know. It echoes with religious intuitions and psychological identity. It is the essence of mind as opposed to machine. It is the source of creativity and free will. If you don't understand it, you may have a theory of computers but you do not have a notion of intelligence… All the AI scenarios assume the premise of AI super-intelligence with anthropomorphic consciousness, will, feelings, imagination, creativity, and independence… The AI experts want to deny it, but until they come to terms with consciousness they cannot explain mind… The blind spot of AI* [i.e., the community of AI enthusiasts] *is that consciousness does not emerge from thought; it is the source of it… A machine by definition lacks consciousness. A machine is part of a determinist order. Lacking surprise or the ability to be surprised, it is self-contained and determined… The 2017 Asilomar conference* [i.e., the Beneficial AI 2017 conference] *called to mind a conference held at the same place in February 1975, at which scientists warned about the future of technology—in that case, genetic engineering… All that the first* [i.e., the 1975] *Asilomar conference managed to achieve was triggering an obtuse paranoia about 'genetically modified organisms'* [i.e., the arrogance and hubris which launched counterproductive and reprehensible international GMO scaremongering] *that hinders agricultural progress around the world… More than four decades later, the hopes and fears of the 1975 Asilomar conference are nowhere near to coming true.*"[20]

---

[20] Gilder, ibid

That is not to say there aren't dissenting voices among the intelligentsia. None other than Peter Thiel—child prodigy, master chess player, self-made billionaire, and author of *ZERO TO ONE: Notes on Startups, or How to Build the Future*—is on record[94] with an opposing view, as follows.

"Google's algorithms assume the world's future is nothing more than the next moment in a random process. George Gilder shows how deep this assumption goes, what motivates people to make it, and why it's wrong: the future depends on human action."

Formidable Geopolitical Adversaries

The geopolitical world has undergone many subtle changes and some not-so-subtle changes since the Cold War era. Some observers have been lulled into believing world wars are things of the past. Sadly, nothing could be farther from the truth. All which has changed with the demise of the former Soviet Union is that a newer and vastly more dangerous adversary has taken its place in the world, and that adversary is China. Among other things, what makes China a much more formidable adversary is its extraordinary cunning and deception. Aided by the enormous complexities of the Mandarin language relative to Indo-European languages and by the woeful ignorance, preconceptions, and naiveté of US government officials, the Chinese have been able to openly conduct their nefarious inequities around the world with little real understanding of their intentions in Western countries. Consider the following apologia by Michael Pillsbury[95]—perhaps the most authoritative China expert in the Western world.

"Many of us who study China have been taught to view the country as a helpless victim of Western imperialists—a notion that China's leaders not only believe, but also actively encourage… This perspective— the desire to help China at all costs, the almost willful blindness to any actions that undercut our views of Chinese goodwill and victimhood— has colored the US government's approach to dealing with China…

One of the first things a student of the Chinese language learns is its essential ambiguity... The language's [i.e., Mandarin's] *very complexity is like a secret code. A foreigner has to make important decisions about how to translate Chinese concepts, which can inherently lead to misunderstandings... Unfortunately, the vast majority of so-called China experts in the United States do not speak Chinese beyond a few words—enough to feign competence in the presence of those who do not speak the language fluently. This fact makes it easier for the supposed China 'experts' to interpret Chinese messages subjectively in ways that conform to their own beliefs. What we all must do better is to look not just at speeches but also at the context of those speeches, and we need to look for larger hidden meanings. For well over a half century, Americans have failed to do this. Until recently, the sometimes vaguely phrased expressions of the Chinese hawks were obscure references to ancient history, so their input to Chinese strategy was hidden from most foreigners... We underestimated the influence of China's hawks. Every one of the assumptions behind that belief was wrong—dangerously so. The error of those assumptions is becoming clearer by the day, by what China does and, equally important, by what China does not do.*

For four decades now, my colleagues and I believed that 'engagement' with the Chinese would induce China to cooperate with the West on a wide range of policy problems. It hasn't. Trade and technology were supposed to lead to a convergence of Chinese and Western views on questions of regional and global order. They haven't. In short, China has failed to meet nearly all of our rosy [i.e., reprehensibly naive] *expectations... In our hubris, Americans love to believe that the aspiration of every other country is to be just like the United States.* [Note the conceit, egocentricity, ignorance and naiveté embodied in this belief.] *In recent years, this has governed our approach to Iraq and Afghanistan. We cling to the same mentality with China. In the 1940s, an effort was funded by the U.S. government to understand the Chinese mind-set. This culminated in several studies, including one in which 150 Chinese emigrants in New York's Chinatown were shown Rorschach inkblot cards. The researchers, who included the scholars Nathan Leites, Ruth Benedict, and Margaret Mead, also analyzed the themes of popular Chinese books and films. One conclusion that emerged was that the Chinese did not view strategy the same way Americans did. Whereas Americans tended to favor direct action, those of Chinese ethnic origin were found to favor the indirect over the direct, ambiguity and deception over clarity and transparency. Another conclusion was that Chinese literature and writings on strategy prized deception... The results of the original 1940s study—the idea that an ethno-national group viewed the world differently—proved controversial and politically incorrect, and they were never published. The sole existing copy rests quietly in the Library of Congress. It would not be until 2000 that I learned from Chinese generals that the study's conclusions were essentially correct.* [Note the horrific social costs of exploiting the false dogma of 'political correctness' as a tool to censor and suppress opposing views.]

Over time, I discovered proposals by Chinese hawks (ying pai) to the Chinese leadership to mislead and manipulate American policymakers to obtain intelligence and military, technological, and economic assistance. I learned that these hawks had been advising Chinese leaders, beginning with Mao Zedong, to avenge a century of humiliation and [that they] *aspired to replace the United States as the economic, military, and political leader of the world by the year 2049 (the one hundredth anniversary of the Communist Revolution). This plan became known as 'the Hundred-Year Marathon.' It is a plan that has been implemented by the Communist Party leadership from the beginning of its relationship with the United States. The goal is to avenge or 'wipe clean' (xi xue) past foreign humiliations. Then China will set up a world order that will be fair to China, a world without American global supremacy, and revise the US-dominated economic and geopolitical world order founded at Bretton Woods and San Francisco at the end of World War II. The hawks assess that China can only succeed in this project through deception, or at least by denial of any frightening plans... Chinese leaders routinely reassure other nations that 'China will never become a hegemon.'... They merely want to restore China to its former global position of three hundred years ago, when it commanded roughly a third of the world economy. That apparently means becoming at least twice as strong as the United States by 2049... Dismissing Chinese nationalism as out of the mainstream is what most Western experts on China have done for decades… And because we have no idea the Marathon is even under way, America* [i.e., the US] *is losing."*[21]

What a shock it must have been for Pillsbury and his US associates to discover that China had been nursing a Hundred-Year Marathon to world domination from the inception of <u>Mao Zedong's</u>[96] Chinese communist government in 1949.

"Liu [i.e., <u>Liu Mingfu</u>[97], a colonel in the People's Liberation Army (PLA) and a former leading scholar at China's National Defense University with responsibility for training future generals of the PLA] *also hints at the existence of an official Marathon strategy among the Chinese leadership, praising Mao Zedong* [the 'founding father' of the Chinese communist revolution] *because 'he dared to craft a grand plan to surpass America, stating that beating the United States would be China's greatest contribution to humanity.'… The China scholar William A. Callahan translates tianxia* [translated from Mandarin as 'under-heaven,' 'empire,' and 'China'] *as a unified global system with China's 'superior' civilization at the top. Other civilizations, such as the United States, are part of the 'barbarian wilderness.' As the center of the civilized world, China would have the responsibility to 'improve' all the nations and peoples of the world by 'harmonizing' them—spreading Chinese values, language, and culture so they can better fit into under-heaven. This empire 'values order over freedom, ethics over law, and elite governance over democracy and human rights.'… I met Zhao Tingyang in Beijing in July 2012, after he had achieved international acclaim. I asked him how the tianxia system would handle disobedience, in case any nations refused to follow the Chinese script. 'Easy question,' he replied. 'The Rites of Zhou prescribed a four-to-one military superiority to enable the emperor to enforce the All-Under-Heaven system.' In other words, after China wins the economic Marathon and develops an economy twice as large as America's, China's new status may have to be protected through*

---

[21] *THE HUNDRED-YEAR MARATHON*[98]*/ China's Secret Strategy to Replace America as the Global Superpower*, by Michael Pillsbury, Henry Holt and Company, Kindle Edition, 2018

military force. The world's largest economy will need a force more powerful than any other—one that would eventually render American military might obsolete... The warnings the Soviet diplomats at the United Nations had provided in 1969 about Beijing's deceptive tactics and long-term global ambition [which had been ridiculed and ignored by the egocentric and ignorant China analysts in the US at the time] *were now coming true."*[22]

Propelled by Pillsbury's seminal understanding, US China policy "experts" are belatedly embracing the harsh reality that execution of its Hundred-Year Marathon over the last sixty-nine years has enabled China to acquire trillions of dollars in US economic, military, and technological aid—aid that has enabled China to increase the size of its economy by a factor of ten in less than fifty years.

"At the time [i.e., 1969], *the Chinese economy was languishing at about 10 percent of America's GNP. It seemed unrealistic that the Chinese would dare to dream about truly surpassing the United States."*[23]

When President Donald Trump[99] says the US has rebuilt China, what he means is that—through a combination of US trade deficits with China and US intellectual property thefts by China—the US has paid for most of the rebuilding, and he is speaking the truth. As illustrated in the chart on page 45, China has enjoyed cumulative trade surpluses with the US of more than $5 trillion since 1985 and—with a few exceptions—the bloodletting has been increasing every year. Note that the data in the chart do not include the trillions of additional dollars lost through China's theft of US intellectual property[100] and, in all likelihood, China has stolen US intellectual property worth at least an additional $5 trillion over the last quarter century. Note too that a $10 trillion transfer of wealth from the US to China translates into a $20 trillion change in the relative economic strengths of the two countries. Can you imagine how

---

[22] Pillsbury, op cit
[23] Pillsbury, ibid

different China and the US would be today if this wholesale fraud and theft had been prevented and those trillions of dollars had been invested in US infrastructure instead of China infrastructure? It's a question that merits an answer.

With unabashed candor and only a hint of embarrassment, Pillsbury states: "*Our decades-long ignorance of China's strategic thinking has been costly; our lack of understanding has led us to make concessions to the Chinese that seem outright senseless in hindsight.*"[24] No kidding! One could say that! After all, what is $10 or $20 trillion between two countries competing for economic and military world dominance?—other than a good possibly that it's the difference between winning and losing. Pillsbury then goes on to explain: "*Undoubtedly, America's ignorance—and that of the West more broadly—can be at least partly attributed to two key factors. First, from the seventeenth century to the modern era, Sinologists, missionaries, and researchers who visited and studied China were essentially led to accept a fabricated account of Chinese history.*"[25] To be kind, this is hardly a satisfactory explanation for what is arguably the greatest failure of statecraft in US history. What it says is that US China "experts" were at least partially basing their interpretations of China policies on centuries old accounts by what can only be regarded as casual China visitors—most of whom had only anecdotal knowledge of China and, in all probability, never developed enough fluency in Mandarin to read Chinese history books of which there are many—as China has more and better written documentation of its history than any other country of similarly ancient origin.

Finally, in an effort to redeem himself, Pillsbury reports that: "*In 1991, China's leaders secretly used a Warring States proverb, tao guang, yang hui. When the document containing this phrase leaked, Beijing translated it as the cryptic and generic 'bide your time, build your capabilities.' BUT IN ITS PROPER CONTEXT, THE PROVERB ACTUALLY ALLUDES TO OVERTURNING THE OLD HEGE-*

---

[24] Pillsbury, ibid
[25] Pillsbury, ibid

MON AND EXACTING REVENGE, BUT ONLY ONCE THE RISING POWER HAS DEVELOPED THE ABILITY TO DO SO [EMPHASIS by author].*"*[26]

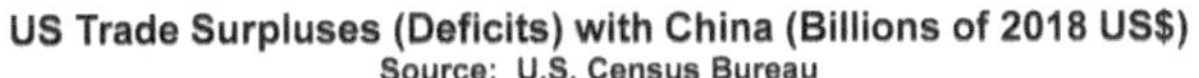
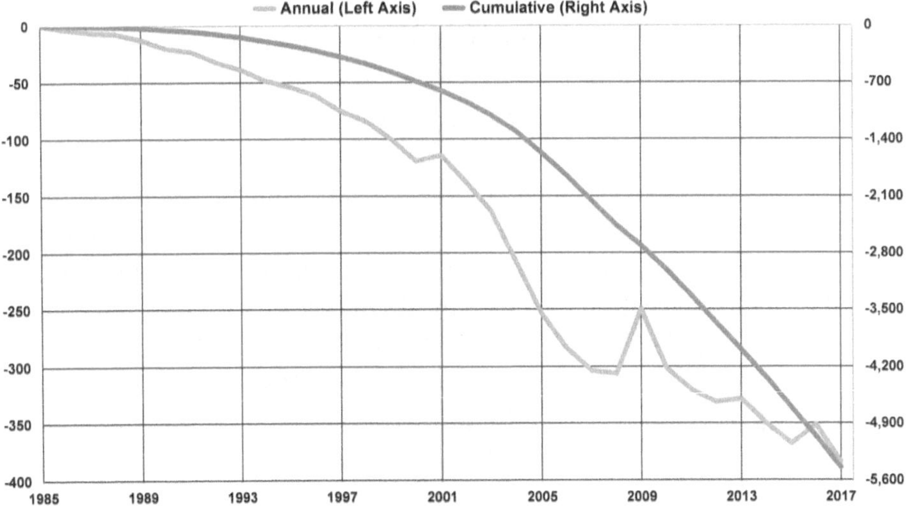

Since 1985, US trade deficits with China have totaled more than $5 trillion, and they have been steadily increasing!

Geopolitical Economic Warfare

As observed by Peter Thiel, "the future depends on human action," and positive proactive human action is desperately needed. Consider what has happened in the US just since World War II. Insidious and seditious Neo-Marxist indoctrination and promotion of multiculturalism by the Neo-Marxist revolutionaries now dominating US educational institutions—coupled with egregiously misguided US immigration policies—have been gradually transforming the US into a quasi Latin American "banana republic[101]" overrun by tens of millions of illiterate and unskilled immigrants—most of whom have only a rudimentary command, if any, of the English language; have little or

---

[26] Pillsbury, ibid

no knowledge of US founding principles and values; have not sworn allegiance to the US Constitution; are not US citizens; and have no clear incentive to assimilate into a common US culture.

During most of this same period, ruinous US economic policies instituted by lobbyists for an unholy alliance of foreign governments and some of the world's largest globalist and mercantilist multinational corporations have systematically ravaged US economic power. With unbridled hubris, the egocentric and supercilious executives who operate such corporations frequently operate them as sovereign "corporate states" with little or no regard for their economic or social impact on the countries in which they operate—including the countries in which they are based.

Consequently, they don't hesitate to exploit their economic and political power to influence economic policies in the countries in which they operate. Nor do they hesitate to move critical industries and resources from one country to another to arbitrage any economic policy and subsidy differences between them. Although somewhat hyperbolic, the following quote demonstrates that the ruinous effects which misguided globalist and mercantilist economic policies are having on the US were already evident to some nearly thirty years ago.

"Today [i.e., in1991, when the US National Debt was only $3.6 trillion vs. $20 trillion in 2017 (both stated in 2018 US$)], *this nation* [i.e., the US] *lies in economic ruins, devastated and destitute, in much the same dire straits in which Germany and Japan found themselves in 1945. Will Americans act to rebuild our nation, as Germany and Japan have done when they faced the identical conditions which we now face—or will we continue to be enslaved by the Babylonian debt-money* [i.e., politically corrupted fiat-money] *system which was set up by the Federal Reserve Act in 1913 to complete our total destruction? This is the only question which we have to answer, and we do not have much time left to answer it."*[27]

---

[27] From the 1991 Forward to *SECRETS OF THE FEDERAL RESERVE*[102] *(The London Connection)* by Eustace Mullins, first published in 1952 by Kasper and

In the last four decades, ill-conceived trade policies have ravaged US manufacturing industries and blue-collar jobs, beggared the middle class, produced nearly $15 trillion (2018 US$) of US trade deficits, and increased the US National Debt by more than $17 trillion (2018 US$)—with a near-perfect correlation of 0.98 since 1960 between the cumulative US trade deficit and the US National Debt. Through 2017, US trade deficits with China alone accounted for more than one-third of the cumulative US trade deficit of $15 trillion (2018 US$) and more than one-fourth of the total US National Debt of more than $20 trillion (2018 US$).

Tragically, the US foreign trade policy blunders of the last four decades were compounded by President Lyndon Johnson's[103] 1964 "War on Poverty[104]," which was supposedly designed to lift aggrieved minorities out of poverty but has had no such effect—even though it has cost the US more than $22 trillion over more than fifty years. What is worse is that this sham "War on Poverty" has been a magnet for attracting tens of millions of illiterate and unskilled illegal immigrants to the US and, as of 2017, this massive invasion has increased social welfare costs to US taxpayers by at least $116 billion per year[105].

Unfortunately, US economic policies in the last four decades have been so ruinous that the US National Debt is now more than 100% of the US gross domestic product[106] or GDP. Indeed, the US is now one of the world's most indebted nations with a debt-to-GDP ratio roughly equal to that of Jamaica and greater than all but nine of one hundred and seventy-four countries. By comparison, in 1945 the US National Debt was a mere $251.43 billion ($3.33 trillion in 2018 US$)—and that after fighting and financing a global war which devastated the economies of all of its other participants.

Given that 84% of the US National Debt has been accrued in the last twenty-five years, one might suspect that information services are responsible for the increase, but that is not the case. In fact,

---

Horton, New York: "*The original book was the first nationally-circulated revelation of the secret meetings of the international bankers at Jekyll Island, Georgia, 1907-1910, at which place the draft of the Federal Reserve Act of 1913 was written.*"

the US enjoys a positive balance of trade in services. Thus, the egregious and unprecedented US trade deficits are <u>entirely due to trade in goods and not services</u>[107]. Moreover, the positive US trade balances in services are now being threatened by escalating cyberespionage and cybernetic warfare.

The Trump Administration is presently engaged in negotiating new trade agreements with all major US trading partners in an effort to stem the bloodletting. If those efforts succeed, the US may yet be restored to some of its former prosperity. On the other hand, if those efforts fail, US prosperity may be further reduced to the point where increased social discord, dysfunction, and instability finally achieve the long-sought-after goal of the Neo-Marxists, namely: the overthrow of constitutional democratic US government and installation of a fascist dictatorship in its place.

A Historic Failure of US Statecraft

For those who have read *HOW DEMOCRACIES PERISH*,[28] Jean-Francois Revel's[108] account of the Kafkaesque fecklessness of Western European countries in their dealings with the former Soviet Union during the Cold War, it's evident China is playing the same game of deception and disinformation that communist states have been playing with democratic states for the last one hundred years. As summarized by Revel, the communist concept of "detente" or accommodation with democratic states is one in which the communist states receive concrete gains from the democratic states in return for vague promises of future internal reforms which they have no intention of honoring. However, China is playing the game far more effectively and proficiently than the Soviet Union ever did. The Soviets—who were not nearly as adept at deception and had a vastly

---

[28] *HOW DEMOCRACIES PERISH*,[109] by Jean-Francois Revel, Harper & Row, Publishers, 1983, chronicles the incredible array of simple-minded geopolitical malfeasances by "Western Democracies" over the 50-year period 1933-1983 – during which time they did just about everything wrong in their dealings with communism and fascism and learned little or nothing from the experience.

more primitive strategy for technologically overtaking the West—were amateurs compared to the Chinese.

Two examples will prove the point. The Soviets never considered sending some of their brightest science, technology, engineering, and mathematics (STEM) students to the US to become expert in advanced US technologies—partly out of unwarranted egocentric hubris and partly out of a warranted fear they would defect. The Soviets did send a lot of espionage agents to the US, but only those who were adults with family members still in the Soviet Union who could be leveraged to prevent defections. By contrast, there currently are an estimated 300,000 Chinese foreign students studying in US colleges and universities—many of whom are graduate STEM students. Moreover, arrogantly believing their own Marxist-Leninist agitprop, the Soviets steadfastly refused to embrace capitalism in any meaningful way, whereas China—having learned from the failed Neo-Marxist model of the Soviet Union—embraced "*'a system termed 'authoritarian capitalism.' Andrew Nathan*[110] *of Columbia University, writing in Journal of Democracy, calls the transformation 'authoritarian resilience.'*"[29]

Interestingly, since the collapse of the Soviet empire, Sino-Russian relations have markedly improved[111]. Evidently, Russia is learning from the greater success of China's system of "authoritarian capitalism" or "authoritarian resilience." Consequently, the US is now faced with not one but two fierce global adversaries both of whom are nursing long-standing grudges against the US and are hell-bent on overthrowing US global economic and military supremacy. This new cold war is a far cry from the "new world order" envisioned by optimists in the West when the Soviet empire collapsed.

Tragically, as acknowledged by Pillsbury: "*The constructive engagement crowd, populated by prominent academics, diplomats, and former presidents, has held significant sway over [US] policymakers and journalists covering China. I should know—I was a member of this group for many decades… We believed that American [i.e., US] aid to a fragile China whose leaders thought like us would help China become a demo-*

---

[29] Pillsbury, ibid

cratic and peaceful power without ambitions of regional or even global dominance."[30] No doubt that was the same "constructive engagement crowd" of China apologists who presided over the cover-up[31] of the fact that it was China who first brought illegal drugs across the Mexican border into the US in the 1960s, thereby initiating a flood of illegal drugs into the US from Mexico and lighting the fuse that ignited the current US pandemic in illegal drug abuse. From the earliest days of the Vietnam War, it was well known to the FBI that China had deployed a small cadre of secret agents to US college and university campuses for the express purpose of supplying free drugs to students who agreed to stage riots in opposition to the Vietnam War. A spectacular success, that secret act of war was undertaken by China to undermine US support for the Vietnam War, as retribution for its defeat by the US in the Korean War, and as retribution for Chinese suffering at the hands of Occidentals in the infamous Opium Wars. Evidently, what goes around, comes back around with dividends.

To his credit, Pillsbury readily admits that it has taken him fifty years to make the transition from his preconception that "*The idea that the future could belong to a Marxist backwater that couldn't even feed its people seemed ridiculous*" to a realization that "*The bias of wishful thinking has created a blind spot to what is likely to emerge as America's thorniest national security challenge in the next twenty-five years.*"[32] Still some who are not embarrassed by an unwitting participation in this colossal and historic failure of US statecraft will consider Pillsbury's assessment of the resulting US national security challenge to be a serious understatement of the true threat posed by a

---

[30] Pillsbury, ibid

[31] The infiltration of Chinese communist agents into US colleges and universities in the 1960s has never been officially acknowledged or exposed by the US government. One can only speculate as to why it has not but, as in the case of the September 11, 2001 massacres, the failed US government bureaucracies involved were greatly embarrassed by the ease with which a foreign enemy was able to infiltrate the US and violate its laws and, in the time-honored tradition of bureaucrats everywhere, rationalized that "what you don't know, won't hurt you" and covered it up to escape accountability.

[32] Pillsbury, ibid

resurgent China—not to mention the many trillions of dollars China already has siphoned from the US due to a combination of its treachery and US stupidity, or the resulting weakening of the US economy and strengthening of the China economy.

To underscore the seriousness of China's Hundred-Year Marathon to world domination, one has only to check out the <u>2018 Annual Report to Congress by the US Department of Defense</u>[112], which reports that China's defense budget of \$154.3B 2017US\$ is more than three times larger than Russia's defense budget of \$48.6B 2017US\$. By comparison, the US defense budget was \$681.1B 2017 US\$. Thrilled as they must be with the success of their sixty-nine-year-long undeclared "stealth war" with the US, Chinese hawks are so confident of their intellectual and ultimate economic superiority over the US they are exhibiting the same kind of egocentricity, hubris, and paranoid xenophobia displayed by Japanese militarists prior to World War II. Fortunately for the US—not to mention the rest of the democratic world—Chinese hawks appear to be as ignorant of Western cultures as we are of theirs. Indeed, they have such contempt and disdain for the US that a few were willing to openly discuss the real Hundred-Year Marathon with Pillsbury. Consequently, he was able to "crack their code"—i.e., cut through the fog of their Mandarin dissimulations—and translate China's Marathon strategy as follows.

"The Marathon strategy that China's leaders are pursuing today—and have been pursuing for decades—is largely the product of lessons derived from the Warring States period by the hawks. The nine principal elements of Chinese strategy, which form the basis of the Hundred-Year Marathon, include the following:

Induce complacency to avoid alerting your opponent. *Chinese strategy holds that a powerful adversary, such as the United States today, should never be provoked prematurely. Instead, one's true intentions should be completely guarded until the ideal moment to strike arrives.*

Manipulate your opponent's advisers. *Chinese strategy emphasizes turning the opponent's house in on itself by winning over influential* *advisers surrounding the opponent's leadership apparatus. Such efforts have long been a hallmark of China's relations with the United States.*

Be patient—for decades, or longer—to achieve victory. *During the Warring States period, decisive victories were never achieved quickly. Victory was sometimes achieved only after many decades of careful, calculated waiting. Today, China's leaders are more than happy to play the waiting game.*

Steal your opponent's ideas and technology for strategic purposes. *Hardly hindered by Western-style legal prohibitions and constitutional principles, China clearly endorses theft for strategic gain. Such theft provides a relatively easy, cost-effective means by which a weaker state can usurp power from a more powerful one.*

Military might is not the critical factor for winning a long-term competition. *This partly explains why China has not devoted more resources to developing larger, more powerful military forces. Rather than relying on a brute accumulation of strength, Chinese strategy advocates targeting an enemy's weak points and biding one's time.*

Recognize that the hegemon will take extreme, even reckless action to retain its dominant position. *The rise and fall of hegemons was perhaps the defining feature of the Warring States period. Chinese strategy holds that a hegemon—the United States, in today's context—will not go quietly into the night as its power declines relative to others. Further, Chinese strategy holds that a hegemon will inevitably seek to eliminate all actual and potential challengers.*

Never lose sight of shi… *For now, suffice it to say that two elements of shi are critical components of Chinese strategy: deceiving others into doing your bidding for you, and waiting for the point of maximum opportunity to strike.*

Establish and employ metrics for measuring your status relative to other potential challengers. *Chinese strategy places a high premium on assessing China's relative power, during peacetime and in the event of war, across a plethora of dimensions beyond just military considerations. The United States, by contrast, has never attempted to do this.*

Always be vigilant to avoid being encircled or deceived by others. *In what could be characterized as a deeply ingrained sense of paranoia, China's leaders believe that because all other potential rivals* *are out to deceive them, China must respond with its own duplicity. In the brutal Warring States period, the naïve, trusting leader was not just unsuccessful in battle; he was utterly destroyed. Perhaps the greatest Chinese strategic fear is that of being encircled. In the ancient Chinese board game of wei qi, it is imperative to avoid being encircled by your opponent—something that can be accomplished only by simultaneously deceiving your opponent and avoiding being deceived by him. Today, China's leaders operate on the belief that rival states are fundamentally out to encircle one another, the same objective as in wei qi."*[33]

By the time we reach middle age most of us have had to deal with people who are wed to erroneous preconceptions but, if fifty years are required to free some people of such preconceptions, one must ask why such people are entrusted with key advisory roles in the US government. Moreover, one must wonder how long it would have taken to correct the counterproductive and disastrous misconception of China's intentions if Pillsbury hadn't become fluent in Mandarin. Or, what would be US China policy today if Pillsbury hadn't lived long enough to overcome his "hubris?" Or, how many fewer trillions of dollars of US "aid" China would have received if it had taken only twenty-five years instead of fifty years for Pillsbury and his associates to overcome their academic egocentricity and ignorance. Or, if Pillsbury—like so many of his colleagues—had lacked the character, courage, and honesty to admit his colossal blunder.

As demonstrated by US China policy over the last half century, the competence of US statesmen in their dealings with China has shown no improvement over that of Western European statesmen in their dealings with the Soviet Union during the Cold War. With China now an even greater threat to international peace and stability than the Soviet Union ever was, Revel's insights[34] make it indelibly

---

[33] Pillsbury, ibid

[34] As an astute observer and a socialist apostate who lived in the heart of Western Europe throughout World War II and the ensuing Cold War, Revel was uniquely qualified to assess European political developments during the Cold War. In *HOW DEMOCRACIES PERISH*, he chronicled how time after time Western European "statesmen" were cowered and duped by the Soviets into act-

clear that the US is alone in its fight against international communist expansionism and certainly can't depend on its so-called "allies." Consequently, it's clear that for the last half century US China policies have been as ill-conceived and counterproductive as Western Europe's Soviet Union policies were during the Cold War.

Farcical World Government

As evidenced by the wholesale cheating on multinational trade agreements among sovereign states which has been on-going for at least four decades, it's indelibly clear the incentive to cheat is so irresistible and politically overwhelming that such agreements are largely unenforceable. Global experience has demonstrated that—in the absence of a single sovereign international government with law-enforcement powers sufficient to compel compliance with international agreements—organizations like the United Nations and the World Trade Organization are almost totally feckless except as platforms for public posturing and feel-good window-dressing by politicians.

Past experience demonstrates that when multiple offenders are confronted with a violation by one of their peers and adjudication of the offense is dependent on a jury of those same peers, any attempted adjudication quickly breaks down into an exercise in diplomatic foot-dragging, negotiating, and posturing which stifles meaningful enforcement on behalf of aggrieved parties. By no coincidence, the Trump Administration has embarked upon a more-enlightened policy of replacing multinational trade agreements with bilateral trade agreements for which enforcement is not dependent on the verdicts of juries comprised of a defendant's fellow coconspirators.

Since the last half of the nineteenth century, the US has been the home base for some of the world's largest multinational corporations. Faced with a Hobbes' choice between costly, incompetent, and

---

ing against their own interests. He laid bare the manifold hypocrisies, incompetence, and political impotence of Western European countries which frustrated their attempts to reconcile their love affair with Neo-Marxism and their fears of domination by the Soviet Union. Along the way, he leaves no doubt that the Cold War was won by the US in spite of its European allies.

politically-corrupt domestic and international regulation—which failed repeatedly during most of the twentieth century due to "<u>regulatory capture</u>[113]"—and laissez-faire free-market capitalism, the US government has largely opted for the latter.

Consequently, while US-based multinational corporations have been the source of much US prosperity and a mainstay of global US technological superiority, in recent decades some have evolved into self-righteous and self-serving globalist and mercantilist "corporate states" evidently believing they are unaccountable to any but themselves.

Inevitably, their enormous political power, regulatory insularity, and self-serving globalism prompts them to pursue policies which frequently are as detrimental to US national interests and sovereignty as those of any foreign adversary. Whether or not the self-exalting and self-serving corporate "elites" operating these "corporate states" are aware of it, any actions taken by US-based corporations to circumvent official US policies or to conspire with foreign corporations or governments to circumvent those policies, border on sedition and would become treasonous if the current economic "cold" war suddenly became a "hot" war.

Interestingly, in *HOW DEMOCRACIES PERISH*, Revel noted how the cupidity of international financial and corporate interests undermined US efforts to curtail Soviet expansionism during the Cold War. Thankfully, during that war, the offending financial and corporate interests included few US-based corporations, as the Cold War was sufficiently proximal to World War II that they retained enough US patriotism to forego profiteering from misguided US policies or those of its Cold War allies.

Alas, the US is not so blessed today, with US-based corporations perfectly willing to profit from its misguided foreign policies. Thus, unless and until these "corporate states" are legally restrained from selling out their country by transferring state-of-the-art technologies to hostile nations like China in return for market access, they will continue to profit from misguided US policies enabling them to do so.

What is worse is that these "corporate states" have repeatedly demonstrated they will abuse their political power to lobby for policies detrimental to US national security and sovereignty. Consequently, their laissez-faire free-market abuses well may need to be reined in by the US government through stricter law enforcement, regulation, or even enactment of new laws to enforce and reinforce US sovereignty over its geopolitical interactions and trade with foreign countries.

Multiculturalism

Human history is replete with examples of genocides and wars which directly or indirectly grew out of humankind's innate fears and suspicions of others who subscribed to cultures different from their own. Yet, in what can be described only as ongoing demonstrations of humankind's egocentricity and ignorance—i.e., their tragic inability to learn what is obvious to any who are unencumbered by willful blindness—modern societies are being torn apart by the strife that inevitably accompanies multiculturalism.

Even if one is entirely ignorant of human history, an examination of today's world reveals that wherever different cultures are brought together in close proximity, the inevitable result is social discord, dysfunction, and instability. While many societal disruptions have been attributed to differences in religion and religious intolerance, religion is just one of many factors provoking multicultural societal disruptions. Unfortunately, where they exist, religious differences provide convenient labels for identifying the warring factions.

Many other factors such as competition for scarce resources and conquest or invasion by a tribe with a manifestly different culture, ethnic customs, diet, dress, language, and rituals unrelated to religion—not to mention innate human territoriality and xenophobia exacerbated by egocentricity and ignorance—are equally important factors provoking multicultural societal disruptions. Thus, while much of the increased terrorism in Western European countries today which has accompanied their invasion by tens of millions of refugees—fleeing poverty-stricken and war-torn countries in the Middle East—can be attributed to religion, religion does not explain many other multicultural societal disruptions.

For example, differences in religion don't explain the pandemic terrorism between drug cartels in Mexico. Nor do they explain the failure to assimilate all African Americans into mainstream US society over the last fifty years. Moreover, prior to their assimilation into a common US culture, US immigrants sharing the same religion—e.g., French, Hispanic, Irish, Italian, and Polish Catholics—had constant turf wars in major US cities where they lived in close proximity to each other. Indeed, similar turf wars rage across the US today between members of different criminal gangs—most with few, if any, discernible ethnic or religious differences.

Recent scientific research illuminating the negative impact of "diversity"—i.e., the PC euphemism for multiculturalism—on social cohesiveness has been largely suppressed by Neo-Marxist PC censorship. For example, a research report[35] by <u>Robert D. Putnam</u>[114] which illuminated the divisive forces unleashed by multiculturalism was so controversial—among the PC Neo-Marxists now dominating the academy—it wasn't published until five years after it was completed.

The abstract of the report states unequivocally that: *"immigration and ethnic diversity tend to reduce social solidarity and social capital. New evidence from the US suggests that in ethnically diverse neighborhoods residents of all races tend to 'hunker down.'"* Leaving nothing to the imagination, Putnam goes on to explain in excruciating detail exactly what he means by "hunker down."

"In areas of greater diversity, our [30,000] *respondents* [located in 41 of the largest metropolitan areas across the US plus a 10% national sample] *demonstrate:*

- *Lower confidence in local government, local leaders and the local news media*
- *Lower political efficacy – that is, confidence in their own influence*

---

[35] <u>*E Pluribus Unum: Diversity and Community in the Twenty-first Century The 2006 Johan Skytte Prize Lecture,*</u>[115] by Robert D. Putnam, Scandinavian Political Studies, Vol. 30   No. 2, 2007

- *Lower frequency of registering to vote, but more interest and knowledge about politics and more participation in protest marches and social reform groups*
- *Less expectation that others will cooperate to solve dilemmas of collective action (e.g., voluntary conservation to ease a water or energy shortage)*
- *Less likelihood of working on a community project*
- *Lower likelihood of giving to charity or volunteering*
- *Fewer close friends and confidants*
- *Less happiness and lower perceived quality of life*
- *More time spent watching television and more agreement that 'television is my most important form of entertainment'* [i.e., more time spent as zombie-like couch potatoes] "

In other words, Putnam's research reveals that the increase in US multiculturalism resulting from uncontrolled immigration over the last half century has been gradually setting the stage for exploitation by Neo-Marxist demagogues and revolutionaries hell-bent on fanning the flames of divisive race-baiting identity politics as a means of fomenting sufficient social discord, dysfunction, and instability to overthrow constitutional democratic US government.

As <u>Byron M. Roth</u>[116] points out, none of this is surprising.

"IN FACT, THE SOCIAL SCIENCE EVIDENCE THAT A HARMONIOUS SOCIETY COMPOSED OF IDENTIFIABLE ETHNIC GROUPS WITH DIFFERENT CULTURAL AND RELIGIOUS BACKGROUNDS CAN BE ARRANGED IS, ALMOST WITHOUT EXCEPTION, NEGATIVE. Has some new type of social engineering appeared which would allow this historic pattern to be broken? Has some new sort of human being been born who will not repeat the follies of his ancestors?...

Perhaps the most troubling failure, at least to date, has been the failure to fully integrate the black descendants of African slaves into American society. While many black Americans have fully assimilated into the American middle and elite classes, a very large number continues to languish in underclass communities whose way of life is alien to most other Americans. Needless to say, this failure is one of the most disturbing problems confronting America and continues to trouble the nation four decades after the exclusion and subjugation of black Americans was repudiated in the Civil Rights Act of 1964, an act supported by a vast majority of Americans of European descent…

Do the very generous social welfare benefits and affirmative action policies of all modern Western societies create different incentives for people to migrate from those who [sic] existed in the past, when migration was far riskier and the chances of success much smaller? <u>Milton Freedman</u>[117], an ardent proponent of open markets, argued that generous welfare benefits were incompatible with a successful immigration policy. HIS POINT WAS THAT WITHOUT THE PROD OF ECONOMIC NECESSITY, THE MOTIVATION TO ASSIMILATE IS SERIOUSLY REDUCED [EMPHASES by author]."[36]

Of course, it well could be argued that the failure to assimilate all African Americans into mainstream US society over the last fifty years was fully intentional. Given that Lyndon Johnson reportedly was elected to the US Senate by votes cast by "<u>the dead, the halt, the missing and those who were unaware that an election was going on</u>[118]," his so-called "War on Poverty" well may have been deliberately designed to ensure future Democrat majorities in US elections by creating what <u>Dinesh D'Souza</u>[119] terms "<u>urban plantations</u>[120]"—i.e., urban ghettos populated by an underclass that is totally dependent on so-called "welfare programs" designed to maintain them in subsistence-level lifestyles and permanent government dependency—where they will be perpetual reservoirs of malcontents duped into supporting their supposed benefactors while perpetually seeking retribution for their perceived misfortune.

Tragically, as summarized by Roth:

"ALMOST ALL POLLS SHOW THAT PEOPLE ARE EXTREMELY CONCERNED BY THESE CHANGES. A poll con-

---

[36] *THE PERILS OF DIVERSITY*[1121]/ *Immigration and Human Nature*, by Byron M. Roth, Washington Summit Publishers, Whitefish, MT, 2010

ducted by the Pew Foundation in 47 countries involving interviews with more than 45,000 people found overwhelming majorities in favor of further restrictions and controls over immigration. These opinions are not limited to people in the West, but are just as strong, and in many cases stronger, in the countries of Asia, Africa, South America, and the Middle East as they are in Europe and the [sic] *North America. THESE VIEWS ARE MORE INFLUENCED BY CONCERNS WITH THE PRESERVATION OF NATIVE CULTURES THAN WITH ATTITUDES TOWARD IMMIGRANTS…citizens of these countries favor further restrictions on immigration by majorities of 75% in England, 68% in France, 62% in Canada and 75% in the United States. In most Western countries, therefore, these results suggest that concern with immigration is not, as is so often charged, based in xenophobia, but rather a concern that the pace of immigration poses a threat to native folkways… IN THE CASE OF THE DOCTRINE OF MULTICULTURALISM AND MASS IMMIGRATION, HOWEVER, THE POLITICAL LEADERS OF BOTH THE LEFT AND THE RIGHT, AND VIRTUALLY ALL ACADEMICIANS, ARE UNANIMOUS IN THEIR SUPPORT. The consequence is that the members of the general public, who are most affected by immigration, have no parties to represent their interests and are left with a powerful sense of disenfranchisement for the simple reason that on issues of immigration they are, in fact, disenfranchised* [something which President Trump is trying to change in the US]. *A case in point is the 2008 United States Presidential elections, where both nominees favored even more liberalized immigration policies than those then in existence, and this in spite of the overwhelming opposition to these policies by the electorate* [EMPHASES *by author*].*"*[37]

This raises the obvious question: How did the US—the citadel of capitalism—come to embrace this blatantly Neo-Marxist policy? Roth explains the seeming contradiction as follows.

"While it is clear why corporations should support liberal immigration policies, why should leftists, who claim to speak for the work-

---

[37] Roth, op cit

ingman? To answer that question requires a brief digression to examine the way in which Marxist thought has been transformed in recent years so as to embrace multicultural doctrine and mass immigration... MULTICULTURALISM, FOR INSTANCE, IS CLEARLY AN OUTGROWTH OF MARXIST THINKING, WITH ETHNIC GROUPS REPLACING ECONOMIC CLASSES AS THE PRIMARY ACTORS IN THE CONFLICT THAT DEFINES MODERN SOCIETIES. Whites of European stock are the oppressor class, and the various less fortunate racial and ethnic groups are the exploited classes. Another important product of Marxist thinking is its disparagement of nationalism and its promotion of global internationalism. It is, perhaps, the driving idea behind the formation of a political European Union, as opposed to a merely economic common market. And it certainly explains the faith of the left in world organizations such as the UN and the World Court. It also explains the left's embrace of large-scale Third-World immigration to the industrial democracies, which serves to dilute white European influence and to reduce distinctions among nation states...

THE ATTACHMENT OF THE MANY INTELLECTUALS TO THIS VIEW EXPLAINS THEIR SUPPORT FOR PROGRAMS OF INTERNATIONAL MULTICULTURALISM THAT DENY ANY DIFFERENCE BETWEEN PEOPLE AND CULTURE. It also explains their concern for the world's oppressed minorities, a concern that trumps their concern for their own countrymen. To favor one's own over others is viewed as a base chauvinism. THEREFORE, THE INCONSISTENCY OF SUPPORTING MASS IMMIGRATION WHILE AT THE SAME TIME CLAIMING A CONCERN FOR THE WORKING POOR DISAPPEARS IF ONE DEFINES THE WORKING POOR IN INTERNATIONAL TERMS, RATHER THAN IN CHAUVINISTIC, [or patriotic] NATIONAL ONES. Put in other terms, a true Marxist should show a concern for all the struggling masses of mankind; to be more concerned for your own working classes is a retrograde nationalism, best eschewed. THIS CHANGE OF FOCUS EXPLAINS, IN LARGE MEASURE, THE LEFT'S ABANDONMENT OF THE WORKINGMAN AND JOINING

WITH CORPORATE INTERESTS ON THE ISSUE OF IMMI-GRATION. It is, of course, also the case that the parties of the left increase their power by importing Third-World immigrants who overwhelmingly become constituents of those parties. THE NET RESULT IS THAT PEOPLE WHO OPPOSE MASSIVE IMMIGRATION HAVE NO PLACE TO TURN FOR SUPPORT ON EITHER THE RIGHT OR THE LEFT OF THE POLITICAL SPECTRUM [EMPHASES by author].*"[38]

Ironically, when they first adopted their "progressive" agenda at the beginning of the twentieth century, US *nouveau riche* were simply trying to protect their family fortunes from the kinds of socialist and communist—i.e., sociocommunist—confiscations which were contemporaneously unfolding in Europe due to the blatant and egregious economic disparities that existed between the aristocracy and the hoi polloi. In *AMERICA'S 60 FAMILIES*[122], Ferdinand Lundberg[123] relates how US *nouveau riche*—like the newly minted oligarchs[124] of modern Russia—quickly moved to acquire protective political power by infiltrating the highest positions in government. They did this by first coopting Ivy League schools and converting them into preparatory schools for their scions through the coercive power of their "philanthropy." Lundberg outlined the process as follows.

"As control of the colleges and universities in America slipped from the hands of the clergy after the Civil War, the pecuniary element eased itself into dominance. The overwhelming presence of bankers as trustees and regents became only logical, however, once the inner pecuniary motivation of the American university was granted, because the endowments, in combination with the philanthropic foundations and church endowments (supervised by essentially the same persons), conferred upon the trustees a large amount of industrial control and voting power as well as strategic supervision over research and studies. The university endowments are really instruments of industrial as well as social control; and,

---

[38] Roth, ibid

like other endowments, are tax-exempt, making possible an ever-enlarging concentration of authority in the hands of the rich." [39]

Once graduated from the newly "prestigious" institutions, scions of the US *nouveau riche*—led by <u>Woodrow Wilson</u>[125] and the "progressive" movement—quickly infiltrated both the academy and government. Thus was born a permanent US aristocracy every bit as corrupt and self-serving as any other. The new US aristocracy continued to grow exponentially throughout the twentieth century and quickly metastasized into today's class of so-called "elites." Lest anyone be laboring under the misapprehension that a so-called "free press" would serve as a check on this kind of corruption by acting as a kind of <u>Fourth Estate</u>[126] as imagined by <u>Thomas Carlyle</u>[127], Lundberg makes it clear that any such notion is nothing but a vain pipedream, to wit:

"JOURNALISM, which shapes, modifies, or subtly suggests public attitudes and states of mind, morbidly attracts the owners of the great fortunes, for whose protection against popular disapproval and action there must be a constantly running defense, direct or implied, specific or general. The protective maneuvers often take the form, in this plutocratic press, of eloquent editorial assaults upon popular yearnings and ideas. The journalism of the United States, from top to bottom, is the personal affair bought and paid for of the wealthy families... Newspapers all over the world exist, and have existed, in the service of economic and political power rather than in that of truth and noble ideals." [40]

It's worth noting that the globalist Neo-Marxist stratagem to bring about Balkanization and disintegration of the US through open borders has many precedents, as the suicidal folly of multiculturalism has been repeated throughout human history. The former Soviet Union provides a recent example. Even though it tried

---

[39] *AMERICA'S 60 FAMILIES* by Ferdinand Lundberg, The Vanguard Press, New York, 1937

[40] Lundberg, op clt

valiantly for nearly seventy years to homogenize its citizens with its Russification[128] process, it was unable to suppress the use of <u>more than one hundred different languages</u>[129] and utterly failed to establish enough of a common culture to prevent its eventual Balkanization and disintegration. Indeed, no empire which ever attempted to span a large number of different cultures—not those of Alexander the Great, the ancient Romans, Genghis Khan, Charlemagne, Saladin, Tamerlane, Napoleon, the Ottomans, Portugal, Spain, Great Britain, the Third Reich, the Soviet Union, nor any other—has ever succeeded in bridging the chasms which separate peoples of different cultures, despite the fact that most bankrupted themselves in failed attempts to do so.

In stark contrast, the US has been unique in its ability to successfully absorb and integrate peoples from many diverse cultural backgrounds—and the only thing which has made that possible until recently has been assimilation of foreign-born citizens through insistence on their acceptance of English as the single official US language and their sworn allegiance to the US Constitution. That singular achievement is now threatened by counterproductive laws based on infantile ignorance of human nature and its derivative globalist Neo-Marxist theories of multiculturalism.

Clearly, some of the best and most recent sociological research confirms what has been repeatedly demonstrated throughout human history, namely: that multiculturalism always has been a source of friction between cultures. When examined objectively, it's clear that multiculturalism has been a cause of much of the world's strife, and that the globalist Neo-Marxist "diversity" farce inevitably leads to Balkanization, political unrest and social discord. Consequently, when Neo-Marxists extoll the virtues of multiculturalism, they are either demonstrating stupendous ignorance of human nature and the real world in which they live, or they are disseminating deliberate PC falsehoods and seditious agitprop for the express purpose of fomenting social discord, dysfunction, and instability in fervid attempts to overthrow constitutional democratic US government and to install a fascist dictatorship in its place.

THE THREAT OF A WORLD WAR III

Will China Reform Before It's Too Late?

With China sixty-nine years into its Hundred-Year Marathon or undeclared "stealth war," the clock is ticking and every other country—especially Taiwan—has reason to be concerned. Those who are old enough to remember World War II and those who are familiar with early twentieth-century world history can't fail to see the parallels between what was happening in Germany and Japan in the 1930s with what is now happening in the US and China. In the US, we have a reincarnation of the 1930s Nazi "Brownshirts[130]"—aided and abetted by demented billionaires and euphemistically calling themselves Antifa[131]—marching in the streets, attacking any who dare to disagree with them, destroying private and public property, proclaiming they are what they are not, and sowing sedition everywhere they go with seeming impunity. In China, we have Chinese militarists—operating under the euphemism "hawks"[41]—hell-bent on a quest for colonial world domination in the same manner as 1930s Japanese militarists and for much the same reasons, namely: a supercilious racial conceit exacerbated by egocentricity, hubris, and paranoid xenophobia.

Will this time be different? With a reincarnation of 1930s Nazi "Brownshirts" operating in the US and an East Asian superpower

---

[41] Lest the reader be deceived by the euphemism "hawks," recall that hawks is an appellation commonly used to contrast with doves, and hawks routinely kill and devour unwary doves.

lusting after world domination—and both largely ignored by those who could intervene to prevent a violent social catharsis, how different is the world today than it was one hundred years ago? To be sure, there are superficial differences. For one, the geopolitical alignments are different. In today's world, the axis powers likely would be reduced to one, namely: China. Of course, the allied powers would be different as well. Once again, Russia would be forced to ally with the US, if only because it shares a long border with China and well knows how China covets Russia's vast Asian resources. Pity the hapless Russians, though they hate the US for having forced the former Soviet Union into bankruptcy and ultimate dissolution, China poses the same threat to Russia as the Third Reich once did. Consequently, every country that was not already a colony of China would be allied with the US.

Unfortunately for China, its attempts to colonize all of East Asia—not to mention the entire non-Chinese world— are doomed to failure, as China has alienated all of its neighbors, including Russia. Curiously, as demonstrated by its vicious crackdowns on domestic multiculturalism, China's leaders demonstrate an understanding of the divisive forces unleashed by multiculturalism, yet—like the Japanese militarists before them—they fail to recognize the contradiction between their domestic policies and their colonial ambitions. For thousands of years China isolated itself behind its Great Wall and its natural mountain and ocean barriers, and it avoided multicultural friction through its cherished isolation. Unfortunately, for China's hopes of world domination, those chickens are now coming home to roost. No non-Chinese country would be an abiding colony of a supercilious hegemon that has only contempt and disdain for any culture but its own. Even if China was successful in occupying its neighbors by force, as Japan was in the years leading up to World War II and was able to retain control over them at the end of a World War III—analogous to what the Soviet Union was able to do in Eastern Europe at the end of World War II—they would face the same inevitable Balkanization which resulted in the ultimate dissolution of the former Soviet Union and Yugoslavia. Even Taiwan, if conquered, eventually would revert to an independent state, as Russian-speaking Belarus did after the collapse of the Soviet empire.

"It is, of course, on such shared cultural values, and other conventions and beliefs, that a nation's cohesion is based, and that make it distinct from other nations."[42]

China's hawks need to wake up to the fact that no people want to be colonized and subjugated by aliens who have only contempt and disdain for their own unique culture—something Islamists have yet to learn as well. Given their spectacular success to date in exploiting an economic windfall from their undeclared "stealth war" with the US to bring China back from the ravages of its <u>War of Liberation</u>[132] and its <u>Great Leap Forward</u>[133], someone should tell the China hawks to declare victory and quit while they're ahead—for, if they persist in their quest for colonial world domination, they surely will go down in Chinese history in infamy similar to that heaped on the Japanese militarists of the twentieth century—as their quest has even less chance of succeeding than that of Imperial Japan, if only because the US will not just sit idly by as a spectator as it did in the 1930s.

Are these realities not obvious to China? If one must judge by its actions over the last sixty-nine years, the answer is: apparently not. How is that possible? The only satisfactory answer must be that—like the pre-World War II Japanese—the Chinese people believe they have been exploited by aliens with no appreciation or understanding of their intrinsic greatness and superior culture. In other words, their pride has been hurt and, like children in a sandbox fighting over the same toy, they are willing to lash out with the fury of a two-year-old child hitting a sandbox companion over the head with a shovel—which is nothing more nor less than a quintessential example of human ego run amok.

---

[42] Roth, ibid

What Happens If It Doesn't?

A "hot" war with China is certainly not necessary, and it certainly would be as counterproductive for the Chinese people as World War II was for the Japanese people. However, a "hot" war with Japan wasn't necessary either, yet it happened. The obstacle to be overcome is the intransigence of people who believe they have been exploited by aliens with no appreciation or understanding of their intrinsic greatness and superior culture—i.e., the obstacle is innate human territoriality and xenophobia exacerbated by egocentricity and ignorance. If China could be persuaded to respect the sovereignty of other countries and refrain from its wholesale espionage and theft of their intellectual property, there is no reason China could not become a respected member of the community of nations. However, in the absence of a single sovereign international government with law-enforcement powers sufficient to compel compliance with international agreements, there is no reason to believe China would honor its agreements—as persuasively demonstrated by its dishonorable sixty-nine-year-long undeclared "stealth war" with the US.

Is a "hot" war with China inevitable? The obvious answer is no. One does not require supernatural powers to realize China could not win such a war. But, unless it can be persuaded to abandon its quest for colonial world domination, the world surely is headed toward a World War III. Will the threat of their annihilation deter them? It certainly did bring the Japanese militarists up short but, If not, then surely humankind are a depraved and fundamentally flawed species that well could be the instruments of their own extinction.

WARNING SIGNS

Flagrant and Persistent Human Immorality

In today's world one doesn't need to be a criminologist, law-enforcement officer, or psychologist to become familiar with human moral weaknesses as mass media are literally awash in them. Sadly, many human moral weaknesses are frequently glamorized in mass media. What dark forces lurk in the human mind to feed our evidently insatiable fascination with, and demand for, media glamorizing human corruption, crime, decadence, depravity, evil, and licentiousness—to say nothing of hideous underground child pornography and smut films? Are those dark forces innate or do they simply reflect parental and educational failures?

As there is little correlation between such human moral weaknesses and an individual's financial or social status—at least in the US, is our fascination with such moral weaknesses just a natural result of human idleness—as reflected in the aphorism "idle hands are the devil's workshop," or does it result from other external factors such as over-population? Interestingly, crime statistics[134]—from thirty-four US cities reaching from Alaska and Hawaii to New England with populations ranging from two-hundred-and-fifty thousand to more than eight million—show crime rates do not depend on the sizes of local populations.

While there is considerable homogeneity among US cities, there is some evidence that human life is cheaper in more densely populated areas. Cases in point are the evident cheapness of human life on the streets of big cities like Chicago[135] and New York City[136]—not to mention even larger and more densely populated foreign cities—as documented in lurid accounts of innocent bystanders and tourists being maimed and murdered on an almost-daily basis in spite of massive spending on law enforcement.

Under the circumstances, one is forced to wonder what is meant by "inhumane." Evidently, much which was thought to be immoral or inhumane in reality turns out to be all-too-human. A prime example of mankind's inhumanity to man is constantly on display in some of the world's largest and most affluent cities—even in the US. For example, homelessness is increasing in <u>New York City</u>[137] as well as all the major cities on the US West Coast, yet more than <u>43% of US billionaires</u>[138] are located in those same areas.

"The nation's homeless population increased this year [i.e., 2017] for the first time since 2010, driven by a surge in the number of people living on the streets in Los Angeles and other West Coast cities. The U.S. Department of Housing and Urban Development released its annual Point in Time count Wednesday, a report that showed nearly 554,000 homeless people across the country during local tallies conducted in January. That figure is up nearly 1 percent from 2016. Of that total, 193,000 people had no access to nightly shelter and instead were staying in vehicles, tents, the streets and other places considered uninhabitable. The unsheltered figure is up by more than 9 percent compared to two years ago. Increases are higher in several West Coast cities, where the explosion in homelessness has prompted at least 10 city and county governments to declare states of emergency since 2015. City officials, homeless advocates and those living on the streets point to a main culprit: the region's booming economy...

The numbers in the report back up what many people in California, Oregon and Washington have been experiencing in their communities: encampments sprouting along freeways and rivers; local governments struggling to come up with money for long-term solutions; conflicts over whether to crack down on street camping and even feeding the homeless... While the overall homeless population in California, Oregon and Washington grew by 14 percent over the past two years, the part of that population considered unsheltered climbed 23 percent to 108,000...

In booming Seattle, for example, the HUD report shows the unsheltered population grew by 44 percent over two years to nearly 5,500...

The homeless service area that includes most of Los Angeles County, the epicenter of the crisis, saw its total homeless count top 55,000 people, up by more than 13,000 from 2016… In the West Coast states, the surge in homelessness has become part of the fabric of daily life. "[43]

Tragically, today Southern California cities bear a greater resemblance to Latin American metropolises—replete with large homeless populations, slums, and surrounding barrios—than they do to the beautiful, clean, modern, and prosperous cities built there in the 1950s when Southern California was home to the backbone of the US aerospace and defense industries. One wonders if this could be another consequence of the $5 trillion give-away to China in the last thirty years. Interestingly, given that nearly one fourth of all US billionaires call California home, one is forced to conclude the super-rich have no compunction whatever about being surrounded by people suffering in misery and poverty while living in the rankest squalor.

Such big-city atrocities stand in stark contrast to the heroic Great Race of Mercy[139] by dog sled teams—in temperatures of fifty or more degrees below zero Fahrenheit—across nearly seven hundred miles of snow-covered ice and wilderness to deliver an antitoxin in time to stop a diphtheria epidemic in Nome, an Alaskan city of less than two thousand people at the time. Other accounts of rugged Alaskans traveling one hundred miles or more under similar conditions to save a single human life are commonplace. Evidently, human life is more precious where it's less plentiful.

Indeed, human life appears to be less precious in the US today than it was when the nation was less densely populated. Whereas so-called "capital crimes" once carried an automatic death penalty,[44] today most are "pleaded down" to lesser offenses. Consequently, even heinous murderers are frequently sentenced to ten or fewer years of confinement, and many convicted murderers are paroled back into

---

[43] *America's Homeless Population Rises for First Time in Years*[140]

[44] For a brilliant defense of the death penalty, see US Supreme Court Justice Antonin Scalia's May 2002 critique[141] of Avery Cardinal Dulles' April 2001 encyclical: *Catholicism & Capital Punishment*[142]

society well before their sentences have expired. The result has been that thousands of convicted murderers have been returned to society, where many of them resume murdering innocents right where they left off when they were incarcerated. As such experienced and practiced killers are no doubt more adept at evading law enforcement, it's little wonder that <u>thirty-six percent of US homicides go unsolved</u>[143]. The unfortunate and deadly practice of releasing convicted killers back into society too often reflects misguided and pusillanimous judges and politically ambitious and weak-kneed prosecutors more interested in embellishing their conviction records than in delivering equitable social justice. The fact that these same prosecutors find the simple threat of the death penalty to be an effective means of coercing murder suspects to admit their guilt in return for avoidance of a death penalty belies the claim that capital punishment is not an effective homicide deterrent.

Unfortunately, using the threat of the death penalty for the sole purpose of coercing plea bargains from murderers is a self-defeating practice. With death sentences so easily avoided, it's not surprising that actual US death sentences are at their <u>lowest level in forty years</u>[144]. Nor is it surprising that threatening to impose a death penalty is increasingly perceived as a hollow threat, which greatly diminishes its value as a deterrent—a result which only murderers, seditionaries, and revolutionaries could love. Whatever their motivation, practices such as these and the contemporaneous popular support for abortion-on-demand at best reflect a bizarre way of evaluating human life and at worst a wanton disregard for its value.

These realities clearly demonstrate a wide disparity in the generosity afforded one human by another as a function of their mutual environment, and they make it increasingly difficult to rationalize any innate human goodness or kindness—even to members of their own immediate families. Unlike Griffith's Pollyannaish pipedream, any credible explication of the human condition necessarily must begin with an honest appraisal of human corruption, crime, decadence, depravity, evil, and licentiousness, as well as a satisfactory explanation of the source and origin of these human behaviors. If they stem from innate human weaknesses and humankind are unable or unwilling to purge themselves of them, how is it possible to be optimistic about the future of humankind? It's a question which demands an answer.

Neo-Marxist Societal Rot in Western Countries

Perhaps, one of the most counterproductive and delusional conceits of Western countries is the notion that somehow, like a "city upon a hill[145]," their societies are the "light of the world[146]." While it may be an effective means to evoke pride among their citizens, those who invoke it should be reminded of the biblical admonition: "Pride goes before destruction, and a haughty spirit before a fall[147]." To set the record straight, consider the following assessments of the Cold War between the former Soviet Union and the NATO countries by Jean-Francois Revel.

"Democracy tends to ignore, even deny, threats to its existence because it loathes doing what is needed to counter them. It awakens only when the danger becomes deadly, imminent and evident. By then, either there is too little time left for it to save itself, or the price of survival has become crushingly high… What we end up with in what is convention-ally called Western society is a topsy-turvy [i.e., upside-down] *situation in which those seeking to destroy democracy appear to be fighting for legitimate aims, while its defenders are pictured as repressive reactionar-ies. Identification of democracy's internal and external adversaries with the forces of progress, legitimacy, and even peace, discredits and paralyzes the efforts of people who are only trying to preserve their institutions…*

Many people now disenchanted with communism continue to rea-son in terms of the respective strengths of the political right and left, terms that date from the days when communism and its totalitarian sponsors still seemed to them to be springs of social progress… All unawares, the 'bourgeois' press, more out of indolence than malice [That contention well could be argued in today's world.], *has largely taken over the after-sales and reconditioning services for the most ramshackle products of Soviet* [i.e., communist] *disinformation… The fundamental lie is surely the association of communism with progress, defense of the poor and the struggle for peace, while all of communism's enemies are identified as 'reactionaries,' 'conservatives' or 'rightists.' This is disinformation's greatest success... We sometimes forget to cite one of the most effective of the many ways mankind has found to commit suicide: utopia... We will never learn that socialism does not begin to work until it is jettisoned... Westerners who favor an effective nuclear deterrent and a verifiable balance of forces are still viewed as 'conservatives,' 'right-wingers,' 'warmongers' or, at best, as 'cold warriors.' Those advocating unilateral disarmament or, at any rate, prior and increasingly juicier concessions to the Soviet Union* [i.e., to communists] *without reciprocal guarantees are considered 'leftists,' generous souls who love peace... Not even they* [i.e., the communists] *believe what they say about us; they know full well what sort of human values they have cultivated in their civilization, but they go on condemning us because, after all, we love to be insulted... On what bases, with what motivation, can freedom be defended when so many opinion molders, educators and thinkers have always, openly or secretly, maintained that our civilization is 'fundamentally bad?'... Many schoolbooks throughout the West are indictments of capitalism, as violently caricatural as they are contemptible scientifically. But defenseless schoolchildren lack the information they would need to read these books critically.*[45]

An Easy Transition to Orwellian Social Engineering

Whereas Gilder characterizes the Neo-Marxism of the "elite" technocracy as growing out of a kind of harmless, naive, and self-exalting ego trip, others are not so generous and believe its true origin is a supercilious conceit that, as self-appointed "elite" members of society, they are ipso facto members of a superior ruling class—which engenders in them a contempt for, if not an outright loathing of, those lacking credentials similar to their own. Given their overwhelming self-importance and self-love, their inculcated Neo-Marxist biases, and their evident disregard for the societal contributions of other humans, some observers recognize that such self-exalting "elites"

---

[45] Revel, op cit

manifest a dangerous predisposition to social engineering. For example, implicit in the following cogent admonition by J. R. Nyquist[148] is the realization that those who have the unmitigated gall to believe they are "redefining what it means to be human" certainly would not hesitate to try to create a utopian social order through social engineering.

"Those who would free us from racism, sexism and classism, seeking to make 'the world as one' fail to realize that humanity isn't perfectible; that any attempt to make men perfect is likely to confuse essential instincts, breaking up whatever workable order we've managed to achieve. One is reminded of the results of socialism – in Russia and the West."[46]

Indeed, oozing as they are with boundless infantile innocence and unfathomable self-confidence and self-righteousness which can be derived only from profound ignorance of human nature and the limitations of their own knowledge, these coddled scions of privilege would impose their worldviews on the remainder of humankind in a heartbeat. Armed only with sterile textbook knowledge of the world in which they live and years of Neo-Marxist indoctrination by failing educational institutions—commandeered long ago by Neo-Marxist subversives hell-bent on legislating their utopian fantasies into existence through Orwellian social engineering, these self-appointed members of a superior ruling class, left to their own devices, would no doubt exhibit the same measures of deference, humanity, and zeal as Maximilien Robespierre[149] in the Reign of Terror[150] during the French Revolution[151] and would create more dystopia than utopia in the process.

---

[46] *How to Immanentize the Eschaton*[152]

PROGNOSIS

Human Destiny: Crisis or Opportunity?

As demonstrated by classic Greek tragedy, even the ancient Greeks were keenly aware of humankind's egocentricity and recklessness, and they evidently believed such innate weaknesses are humanly insurmountable. The plot lines of Greek tragedies invariably follow a cycle from new-found wealth to personal ruin. Sometimes outlined as[153]: wealth and misapplied prosperity (*olbos*); followed by overabundance (*koros*); followed by arrogance, insolence, and wanton disregard for others (*hubris*); followed by recklessness and madness (*atë*); followed by divine retribution (*nemesis*); the cycle bears an all-too-familiar resemblance to modern human experience.

Nothing illustrates humankind's egocentricity and recklessness better than their misguided search for extraterrestrial intelligence (SETI[154]). What motivates a species which knows it treats what it deems to be less-intelligent earthly life-forms either as food, pests, or pets, to believe any intelligent extraterrestrial life-forms[155] it might encounter anywhere in the universe will be capable of only benign behavior and will pose no threat to itself? Surely, in the best case, any intelligent extraterrestrial life-form given familiarity with humanity's incompetent and irresponsible stewardship of its home planet at minimum would regard humankind as a pestilence to be quarantined as a precautionary measure to prevent their spreading further in the cosmos. In the worst case, any such life-form given that same familiarity at maximum might regard humankind as a source of pets to be subdued—i.e., enslaved, as a source of food to be farmed and harvested, or as pests to be exterminated.

Must past be prologue forever for humankind? Have we learned nothing from our predecessors? If so, what is it about humankind which makes us incapable of learning from the mistakes and successes of our predecessors? And, how is it that humans can deny and ignore grim realities which threaten their own survival? Are humankind intrinsically suicidal as the proverbial lemmings[156] are alleged to be? Are humankind so unable to control their emotions they're capable of mass suicide? The suicides of thousands of Japanese men, women and children[157] at Saipan during World War II are enough to make one wonder. How intelligent is a species that keeps repeating the same disastrous mistakes made by preceding generations of the same species? Just because evolution did not equip humankind with a cumulative memory of their entire history across generations in no way excuses this grievous and potentially fatal error, as the invention of written human language has provided sufficient means to pass down to succeeding generations that which was learned along the way.

Can a species which is so contemptibly self-indulgent and pitifully egocentric, ignorant, reckless, and lacking in self-discipline and self-respect that its members can't refrain from polluting their own bodies with noxious chemicals and powerful addicting drugs be expected to save themselves from accidental suicides and extinction? Objective observers are forced to wonder. Will humanity bring itself to extinction as the inevitable consequence of an inability to control and manage its innate animalistic impulses? Or, will humanity be able to curb its egocentricity sufficiently to halt its social regressions and halt—or even reverse—its habitat destruction? Or, instead, will humankind evolve into the marauding space travelers of science fiction—traveling from one planet to the next only to despoil each to such an extent they are eventually forced to find another?

Science fiction writers have long been fascinated with how humankind and human governance will evolve in the distant future. Most of their stories project continued human social discord, dysfunction, and instability. What, if anything, does this say about humankind's future prospects? At best, it suggests that a majority of science fiction writers are not optimistic about humankind's ability to control their innate animalism, and consequently, they are not optimistic about humankind's distant future. It's easy to see from where science fiction writers draw the inspiration for their dire apocalyptic visions of human evolution. One needs only reflect on human history to see how easy it is for human societies to descend into living hells.

Interestingly, in some languages (e.g., Arabic and Chinese) the words "crisis" and "opportunity" share a common root and are treated as synonyms. Even occidentals can agree that mismanaged opportunities are de facto crises for those who would have benefited from better-managed resolutions, and—as avid acolytes of Alinsky[158] well know—every crisis represents an opportunity for demagogues—a.k.a. "community organizers." So, perhaps humankind's potential impact on their own destiny can be characterized as both a crisis and an opportunity.

Are Humans Destined to Continue Repeating Their Tragic History?

Humanity's tragic history seems to favor Einstein's dire assessment that, as a consequence of its innate animalism, humanity is destined to suffer a perpetual series of feckless attempts to preserve its human rights. What is worse is that humanity's egocentricity and ignorance—as demonstrated by its historical insolent and wanton disregard for judicious long-term management of its natural resources—put survival of its own species at risk. Thus humans well could be the instruments of their own extinction.

For nearly two hundred years, astute and erudite observers of the human condition have warned that human egocentricity and ignorance form a terrible combination which threatens the stability of the social order, if not extinction of the human species per se. Driven by ego and its underlying animalistic insecurities, humans seek to maximize security for themselves, and—in their constant quests to do so—they seek to acquire as much power and prestige for themselves as they can, as quickly as they can.

"While man is being instigated by the love of power—a passion visible in an infant, and common to us even with the inferior animals—he will seek personal superiority in preference to every matter of a general concern; or at best, he will employ himself in advancing the public good, as the means of individual distinction and elevation: he will promote the interest of the state from the selfish but most useful passion of making himself considerable in that establishment which he labors to aggrandize. Such is the true picture of man as a political agent."[47]

"Paradoxically enough, the release of initiative and enterprise made possible by popular self-government ultimately generates disintegrating forces from within. Again and again after freedom has brought opportunity and some degree of plenty, the competent become selfish, luxury-loving, and complacent; the incompetent and the unfortunate grow envious and covetous, and all three groups turn aside from the hard road of freedom to worship the Golden Calf of economic security. The historical cycle seems to be: from bondage to spiritual faith; from spiritual faith to courage; from courage to liberty; from liberty to abundance, from abundance to selfishness; from selfishness to apathy, from apathy to dependency; and from dependency back to bondage once more."[48]

In the twenty-first century even educators, journalists, and their coterie of self-proclaimed analysts, authorities, consultants, and pundits or so-called "experts"—charged with the responsibility for keeping the public informed—seem to be largely ignorant of circumstances and events which occurred prior to their own lifetimes. With depressingly few exceptions, their shallow analyses and commentaries leave the impression their real-world knowledge is limited to their own parochial views of circumstances and events which occurred during and after their own adolescence.

Does this collective ignorance of human history simply reflect failures of human parental and educational institutions, or does it

---

[47] *UNIVERSAL HISTORY*[159] (from the Creation of the World to the Beginning of the Eighteenth Century), by Alexander Fraser Tytler, Volume I, Hilliard, Gray & Company, 1839

[48] Prentis, ibid

reflect a tragic innate human weakness? The former proposition portends dire consequences for humankind unless they can rise to the challenge of correcting the mistakes which have led to their parental and educational failures. Alternatively, if the latter proposition is correct, then humankind have at least one fateful and uncorrectable weakness; Einstein, <u>Tytler</u>[160], and Prentis were right; and humanity is destined to perpetually cycle through periods of social progress and social regression. In either case, the implications for survival of the human species are profound.

Humans appear to be incapable of learning from the mistakes and successes of their predecessors and, unless this pattern is broken, they can look forward only to a dismal future riven by crimes, wars, and social regressions in which human societies continuously cycle through successive periods of social discord, dysfunction, instability, revolution, and counterrevolution. If we accept the erudite wisdom of Einstein, Tytler, and Prentis, it's evident that human egocentricity and ignorance will continue to have profound adverse political and social consequences for humankind. Moreover, if their assessments are correct, there can be but one explanation—more or less as outlined in the following syllogism.

- There always will be inequalities between the capabilities of individual humans which will ineluctably lead to inequalities in their acquisition of human comforts.
- There always will be demagogues ready and willing to exploit any natural inequalities between humans as a means to gain political power for themselves.
- Consequently, there always will be political polarizations among humans created by demagogues exploiting identity politics for their own political gain.
- Consequently, there always will be social discord, dysfunction, and instability in human societies.
- Consequently, there always will be recurrent periods of social progress and social regression as human societies continuously cycle through successive periods of social discord, dysfunction, instability, revolution, and counterrevolution.

Whether or not such cycles would conform to Prentis' "historical cycle" is entirely moot. (His own definition of that cycle is known to have evolved[161].) What is not moot is that there certainly would be recurrent periods of social progress and social regression as was so persuasively demonstrated by the French Revolution, the American Revolution[162], and the Russian Revolution[163]—not to mention many others. The only alternative would seem to be a new American Enlightenment[164] in which the US rises to the challenge and shakes off the debilitating effects of the last one hundred years of its flirtation with the dark forces of Neo-Marxism. Is this still a possibility, or has Neo-Marxism become so firmly embedded in US educational and governmental institutions that it's no longer possible to purge them of this plague? The answer to that question will determine whether or not the US will continue down the path of Prentis' "historical cycle."

On a more optimistic note, disenfranchisement of the US electorate through usurpation of states' rights by the US federal government has inspired a call for a convention of all fifty of the US states to draft much needed amendments to the US Constitution which would rein in the out-of-control, self-appointed, self-aggrandizing, self-perpetuating, self-righteous, and self-serving bureaucracies that have commanded US educational and governmental institutions for most of the last one hundred years.

If the COS Action[165] initiative is successful, the US well could emerge from the last one hundred years of its flirtation with the dark forces of Neo-Marxism possessed of the renewed vigor needed to lead the world out of its current societal rot into a new era of economic and social progress based on the greatest force for human liberty the world has yet conceived, namely: US founding principles and values.

It's not too much to hope for, and it would be a major achievement in postponing, if not preventing, further descent into the kinds of increasingly destructive and devastating Neo-Marxist totalitarian experiments that already have directly or indirectly caused the unnatural deaths of an estimated one hundred million people in the last century alone.

ENDNOTES

1   https://en.wikipedia.org/wiki/What%27s_past_is_prologue
2   https://www.alleydog.com/glossary/definition.php?term=Ego
3   https://www.alleydog.com/glossary/definition.php?term=Self
4   https://en.wikipedia.org/wiki/End_time
5   https://www.alleydog.com/glossary/definition.php?term=Superego
6   https://en.wikipedia.org/wiki/Sturmabteilung
7   https://en.wikipedia.org/wiki/Pope_Benedict_XVI
8   https://www.wtmnewzealand.com/world-transformation-movement/
9   https://en.wikipedia.org/wiki/Jeremy_Griffith
10 http://www.ncregister.com/blog/benjamin-wiker/benedict-vs.-the-dictatorship-of-relativism
11 https://www.google.com/search?ei=tlcxW-3OMszesAWf45OIBQ&q=h.+g.+wells&oq=h.+g.+wel&gs_l=psy-ab.1.0.0l10.6696.8917.0.11380.9.9.0.0.0.0.232.940.6j2j1.9.0..2..0...1.1.64.psy-ab..0.9.936...0i67k1j0i131i67k1j0i131k1.0.V4quq8lThgU
12 https://en.wikipedia.org/wiki/The_Time_Machine
13 https://en.wikipedia.org/wiki/Albert_Einstein
14 https://www.humancondition.com/freedom-essays/the-explanation-of-the-human-condition/
15 https://books.google.com/books?id=8KFNIwjq8HgC&pg=PA60&lpg=PA60&dq=einstein+%2B+%22the+ideals+concerning+the+conduct%22&source=bl&ots=HYPetrfHzS&sig=spJszDXamNqLH_Rv2C3gRL2-3hs&hl=en&sa=X&ved=0ahUKEwjsndCo--XbAhVumK0KHVhsAQ4Q6AEIPDAD#v=onepage&q=einstein%20%2B%20%22the%20ideals%20concerning%20the%20conduct%22&f=false
16 https://en.wikipedia.org/wiki/Sigmund_Freud
17 https://study.com/academy/lesson/the-ego-definition-examples-quiz.html
18 https://en.wikipedia.org/wiki/Laozi
19 https://www.azquotes.com/quote/529622
20 https://en.wikipedia.org/wiki/Bellum_omnium_contra_omnes
21 https://en.wikipedia.org/wiki/Balkanization
22 https://en.wikipedia.org/wiki/Jean_Piaget
23 https://en.wikipedia.org/wiki/Id,_ego_and_super-ego
24 https://www.brainyquote.com/quotes/jean_piaget_751096

25   https://www.biblegateway.com/passage/?search=Proverbs+13%3A24-25&version=KJV

26   http://www.thisdayinquotes.com/2010/11/spare-rod-and-spoil-child-is-not-in.html

27   https://en.wikipedia.org/wiki/Benjamin_Spock

28   https://www.ncbi.nlm.nih.gov/pmc/articles/PMC4358932/

29   http://blogs.lse.ac.uk/usappblog/2016/09/05/religion-is-in-decline-in-the-west-and-america-is-no-exception/

30   https://en.wikipedia.org/wiki/Henning_Webb_Prentis_Jr.

31   http://ergo-sum.net/literature/CultOfCompetency.pdf

32   https://en.wikipedia.org/wiki/Karl_Marx

33   https://en.wikipedia.org/wiki/Educational_attainment_in_the_United_States

34   https://www.amazon.com/Life-After-Google-Blockchain-Economy/dp/1621575764

35   http://www.1517fund.com/

36   https://en.wikipedia.org/wiki/Peter_Thiel

37   https://en.wikipedia.org/wiki/George_Gilder

38   https://books.google.com/books?id=GWEUS3WWXQoC&pg=PA241&dq=change+in+average+marriage+age+in+us&hl=en&sa=X&ved=0ahUKEwiA-OnYxr3cAhVBR6wKHR81BG4Q6AEIRzAF#v=onepage&q=change%20in%20average%20marriage%20age%20in%20us&f=false

39   http://www.npr.org/templates/story/story.php?storyId=141164708

40   https://en.wikipedia.org/wiki/Lord_of_the_Flies

41   https://en.wikipedia.org/wiki/And_the_Children_Shall_Lead

42   http://psycnet.apa.org/doiLanding?doi=10.1037%2Fa0022409

43   https://modelsofmaturityblog.wordpress.com/2016/12/01/the-effect-of-maturity-on-personality-trait-stability/

44   https://www.researchgate.net/publication/244473361_Cupellation_The_oldest_quantitative_chemical_process

45   https://www.history.com/topics/dust-bowl

46   http://www.columbia.edu/~tmt2120/introduction.htm

47   https://en.wikipedia.org/wiki/Chernobyl_Exclusion_Zone

48   https://en.wikipedia.org/wiki/List_of_environmental_disasters

49   https://en.wikipedia.org/wiki/Megafauna

50   https://en.wikipedia.org/wiki/Dodo

51   https://en.wikipedia.org/wiki/Passenger_pigeon

52   https://en.wikipedia.org/wiki/American_bison

53   http://www.iucnredlist.org/details/10269/0

54   http://www.iucnredlist.org/details/10264/0

55   https://www.worldwildlife.org/species/directory?direction=desc&sort=extinction_status

56   https://en.wikipedia.org/wiki/History_of_Easter_Island

57. https://www.smithsonianmag.com/travel/the-mystery-of-easter-island-151285298/

58. http://channel.nationalgeographic.com/u/kckMOO8vzgE0eWAkNc12wFhH8mYhEdkzBsTExn5fwbg3me9RHKoeX6H2XwJHE_46UuQx5Q/

59. https://www.livescience.com/22728-pollution-facts.html

60. https://en.wikipedia.org/wiki/Space_debris

61. https://en.wikipedia.org/wiki/Religious_war

62. https://www.thoughtco.com/albert-einstein-quotes-on-life-after-death-249855

63. https://www.google.com/search?source=hp&ei=RINbW-SuGoPwsAWP8I6YDQ&q=islamist+definition&oq=islamist&gs_l=psy-ab.1.1.0l10.1044.2375.0.10302.8.8.0.0.0.0.109.601.7j1.8.0....0...1c.1.64.psy-ab..0.8.600...0i131k1j0i10k1.0.L873P7D3Ou4

64. https://www.thoughtco.com/european-witch-hunts-timeline-3530786

65. https://en.wikipedia.org/wiki/The_Holocaust

66. https://en.wikipedia.org/wiki/Nazi_Germany

67. https://en.wikipedia.org/wiki/Divine_providence

68. https://www.youtube.com/watch?v=Cf2nqmQIfxc

69. https://www.wsj.com/articles/100-years-of-communismand-100-million-dead-1510011810

70. https://en.wikipedia.org/wiki/Charles_Krauthammer

71. http://www.aei.org/publication/quotation-of-the-day-on-american-exceptionalism/

72. https://en.wikipedia.org/wiki/Thomas_Jefferson

73. http://tjrs.monticello.org/letter/100

74. https://en.wikipedia.org/wiki/Agitprop

75. https://en.wikipedia.org/wiki/Newton_N._Minow

76. https://en.wikipedia.org/wiki/Vladimir_Lenin

77. http://www.heretical.com/miscella/dinform.html

78. https://en.wikipedia.org/wiki/Adolf_Hitler

79. https://en.wikipedia.org/wiki/Saul_Alinsky

80. https://www.youtube.com/watch?v=Cf2nqmQIfxc

81. https://www.amazon.com/Draining-Swamp-David-L-Stein-ebook/dp/B078GZBW9B/ref=sr_1_1?ie=UTF8&qid=1513801500&sr=8-1&keywords=draining+the+swamp+stein

82. https://en.wikipedia.org/wiki/Thomas_Carlyle

83. https://en.wikipedia.org/wiki/Fourth_Estate

84. https://en.wikipedia.org/wiki/Communist_International

85. http://www.heretical.com/miscella/dinform.html

86. https://futureoflife.org/bai-2017/

87. https://futureoflife.org/

88. https://www.booking.com/searchresults.html?aid=311088;label=asilomar-conference-grounds-ue_NSZ%2ASxr1EKKWhMqdHvQS162175

084718%3Apl%3Ata%3Ap1%3Ap2%3Aac%3Aap1t1%3Aneg%3
Afi%3Atikwd-425720713%3Alp9028321%3Ali%3Adec%3Adm;
sid=f1bf592c10ec12a9a87c7e3cc961061f;city=20015036;expand_
sb=1;highlighted_hotels=177269;hlrd=no_dates;keep_
landing=1;redirected=1;source=hotel&gclid=EAIaIQobChMI6eOY
Pi33AIVQ7jACh1EUA3qEAAYASAAEgKwIvD_BwE&

89 https://en.wikipedia.org/wiki/William_F._Buckley_Jr.

90 https://en.wikipedia.org/wiki/Charles_Darwin

91 https://en.wikipedia.org/wiki/Stephen_Hawking

92 https://en.wikipedia.org/wiki/Don%27t_be_evil

93 https://burningman.org/

94 https://www.amazon.com/Life-After-Google-Blockchain-Economy/
dp/1621575764

95 https://en.wikipedia.org/wiki/Michael_Pillsbury

96 https://en.wikipedia.org/wiki/Mao_Zedong

97 https://en.wikipedia.org/wiki/Liu_Mingfu

98 https://www.amazon.com/s?url=search-alias%3Daps&field-keywords=the+h
undred+year+marathon&sprefix=the+hundred+year+m%2Caps%2C208&cr
id=ADQ615AOT5RM

99 https://en.wikipedia.org/wiki/Donald_Trump

100 https://www.theamericanconservative.com/articles/the-unreal-scope-of-
chinas-intellectual-property-theft/

101 https://en.wikipedia.org/wiki/Banana_republic

102 http://www.apfn.org/apfn/reserve.htm

103 https://en.wikipedia.org/wiki/Lyndon_B._Johnson

104 http://www.washingtontimes.com/news/2014/may/21/editorial-
the-not-so-great-society/

105 http://www.irli.org/single-post/2017/09/27/New-FAIR-Study-Illegal-
Immigration-Costs-116-billion-Annually?gclid=EAIaIQobChMIv-v1sZHh3
AIVD4hpCh20nAV2EAAYASAAEgIIVfD_BwE

106 https://tradingeconomics.com/country-list/government-debt-to-gdp

107 https://www.stlouisfed.org/on-the-economy/2017/june/us-trade-deficit
-driven-goods-services

108 https://en.wikipedia.org/wiki/Jean-Fran%C3%A7ois_Revel

109 https://www.amazon.com/s/ref=nb_sb_noss_1?url=search-alias%3Ddigital-
text&field-keywords=how+democracies+perish&rh=n%3A133140011%2C
k%3Ahow+democracies+perish

110 https://en.wikipedia.org/wiki/Andrew_J._Nathan

111 https://en.wikipedia.org/wiki/Sino-Russian_relations_since_1991

112 https://media.defense.gov/2018/Aug/16/2001955282/-1/-1/1/2018-
CHINA-MILITARY-POWER-REPORT.PDF

113 https://en.wikipedia.org/wiki/Regulatory_capture

114 https://en.wikipedia.org/wiki/Robert_D._Putnam

115 https://macaulay.cuny.edu/eportfolios/benediktsson2013/files/2013/04/Putnam.pdf

116 https://www.goodreads.com/author/show/1580448.Byron_M_Roth

117 https://en.wikipedia.org/wiki/Milton_Friedman

118 https://www.nytimes.com/1990/02/11/us/how-johnson-won-election-he-d-lost.html

119 https://en.wikipedia.org/wiki/Dinesh_D'Souza

120 https://theindependentwhig.com/2016/09/01/the-urban-plantation/

121 https://www.amazon.com/s/ref=nb_sb_ss_fb_1_19/140-0417303-3523906?url=search-alias%3Dstripbooks&field-keywords=the+perils+of+diversity&sprefix=the+perils+of+diver%2Cdigital-text%2C198&crid=5YS1L82DKUHJ

122 http://www.freethechurch.org/Library/America's 60 Families.pdf

123 https://en.wikipedia.org/wiki/Ferdinand_Lundberg

124 https://en.wikipedia.org/wiki/Russian_oligarch

125 https://en.wikipedia.org/wiki/Woodrow_Wilson

126 https://en.wikipedia.org/wiki/Fourth_Estate

127 https://en.wikipedia.org/wiki/Thomas_Carlyle

128 https://en.wikipedia.org/wiki/Russification

129 https://en.wikipedia.org/wiki/Languages_of_the_Soviet_Union

130 http://insider.foxnews.com/2017/08/05/antifa-protesters-closest-thing-nazi-brownshirts-dinesh-dsouza

131 https://en.wikipedia.org/wiki/Antifa_(United_States)

132 https://en.wikipedia.org/wiki/Chinese_Communist_Revolution

133 https://en.wikipedia.org/wiki/Great_Leap_Forward

134 https://en.wikipedia.org/wiki/List_of_United_States_cities_by_crime_rate

135 https://en.wikipedia.org/wiki/Crime_in_Chicago

136 https://en.wikipedia.org/wiki/Crime_in_New_York_City#1990s

137 https://www.statista.com/chart/6949/the-us-cities-with-the-most-homeless-people/

138 https://en.wikipedia.org/wiki/List_of_U.S._states_by_the_number_of_billionaires

139 https://en.wikipedia.org/wiki/1925_serum_run_to_Nome

140 https://www.usnews.com/news/us/articles/2017-12-06/us-homeless-count-rises-pushed-by-crisis-on-the-west-coast

141 https://www.firstthings.com/article/2002/05/gods-justice-and-ours

142 https://www.firstthings.com/article/2001/04/catholicism-capital-punishment

143 https://ucr.fbi.gov/crime-in-the-u.s/2013/crime-in-the-u.s.-2013/offenses-known-to-law-enforcement/clearances/clearancetopic_final

144 https://deathpenaltyinfo.org/50-Facts

145 https://en.wikipedia.org/wiki/City_upon_a_Hill

146 https://en.wikipedia.org/wiki/Light_of_the_World

147 https://www.biblegateway.com/passage/?search=Proverbs+16%3A18&version=KJV

[148] http://www.jrnyquist.com/

[149] https://en.wikipedia.org/wiki/Maximilien_Robespierre

[150] https://en.wikipedia.org/wiki/Reign_of_Terror

[151] https://www.thoughtco.com/consequences-of-the-french-revolution-1221872

[152] https://www.financialsense.com/jr-nyquist/how-immanentize-eschaton

[153] http://www.strike-the-root.com/koros-to-hubris-to-ate-to-nemesis

[154] https://www.seti.org/

[155] http://www.space.com/34184-stephen-hawking-afraid-alien-civilizations.html

[156] https://www.britannica.com/story/do-lemmings-really-commit-mass-suicide

[157] https://en.wikipedia.org/wiki/Suicide_Cliff

[158] http://supertradmum-etheldredasplace.blogspot.com/2012/09/saul-alinskys-rules-for-radicals-do.html

[159] https://books.google.com/books?id=2h1LAQAAMAAJ&pg=PA219&lpg=PA219&dq=%22nothing+better+than+an+Utopian+theory,+a+splendid+chimera,+descriptive+of+a+state+of+society+that+never+did,+and+never+could+exist%22&source=bl&ots=_57tUunq3X&sig=Vmohx-qe2rnTdt7nclFczLzcL3A&hl=en&sa=X&ved=0ahUKEwip6aPcorvQAhVO1GMKHZs0AVMQ6AEIGzAA#v=onepage&q=%22nothing%20better%20than%20an%20Utopian%20theory%2C%20a%20splendid%20chimera%2C%20descriptive%20of%20a%20state%20of%20society%20that%20never%20did%2C%20and%20never%20could%20exist%22&f=false

[160] https://en.wikipedia.org/wiki/Alexander_Fraser_Tytler,_Lord_Woodhouselee

[161] http://www.lorencollins.net/tytler.html

[162] http://www.ushistory.org/us/12.asp

[163] http://academic.mu.edu/meissnerd/russian-rev.htm

[164] https://en.wikipedia.org/wiki/American_Enlightenment

[165] https://conventionofstates.com/frequently-asked-questions

ABOUT THE AUTHOR

David L. R. (Dave) Stein,

Serial Entrepreneur (retired)

Dave Stein lives in Austin, Texas. He is a computer-industry and start-up veteran. Over the last fifty years Dave has been a director of ten high-technology start-up companies, including four with combined revenues of more than $1 billion that he cofounded. His track record includes twenty years in the computer industry in a variety of engineering, sales, marketing, and general management positions at Control Data, IBM, Scientific Data Systems, Univac, Systems Engineering Laboratories, and Harris Corporation. In 1979, he cofounded Gartner Inc. where he managed all operations from day one, grew recurring revenues to $40 million in six years, and established Gartner's franchise as the global leader in strategic IT consulting services. In 1985, he cofounded a $250 million venture-capital partnership in Southern California. From 1992 to 2004, he was a management consultant in San Jose. From 2004 to 2016, he was cofounder of two start-up software companies. He received a BS degree with distinction in Mathematics and Physics and did graduate work in Mathematics at the University of Minnesota Institute of Technology.